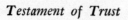

Testament of Trust

BOOKS BY FAITH BALDWIN

Three Women
Departing Wings
Alimony
The Office-Wife
The Incredible Year
Make-Believe
Today's Virtue
Skyscraper
Week-end Marriage
District Nurse
Self-made Woman
Beauty
White-Collar Girl
Love's a Puzzle
Innocent Bystander
Wife versus Secretary
Within a Year
Honor Bound
American Family
The Puritan Strain
The Moon's Our Home
Private Duty
The Girls of Divine Corners
Men Are Such Fools!
That Man Is Mine
The Heart Has Wings
Twenty-four Hours a Day
Manhattan Nights
Enchanted Oasis
Rich Girl, Poor Girl
Hotel Hostess
The High Road
Career by Proxy
White Magic

Station Wagon Set
Rehearsal for Love
"Something Special"
Letty and the Law
Medical Center
And New Stars Burn
Temporary Address: Reno
The Heart Remembers
Blue Horizons
Breath of Life
Five Women in Three Novels
The Rest of My Life with You
Washington, U.S.A.
You Can't Escape
He Married A Doctor
Change of Heart
Arizona Star
A Job for Jenny
No Private Heaven
Woman on Her Way
Sleeping Beauty
Give Love the Air
Marry for Money
They Who Love
The Golden Shoestring
Look Out for Liza
The Whole Armor
The Juniper Tree
Face Toward the Spring
Three Faces of Love
Many Windows
Blaze of Sunlight
Testament of Trust

POETRY

Sign Posts
Widow's Walk

Testament of Trust

by

Faith Baldwin

Holt, Rinehart and Winston

New York

THE AUTHOR ACKNOWLEDGES WITH THANKS
THE PERMISSION TO INCLUDE IN THIS BOOK
MANY OF THE ESSAYS
WHICH WERE ORIGINALLY PUBLISHED IN
Woman's Day UNDER THE TITLE,
"THE OPEN DOOR."

For Alma Lycett, with love.

A FAITHFUL FRIEND IS THE MEDICINE OF LIFE.
Aprocrypha; The Wisdom of Solomon; vi.16

Foreword

A year is like a new house; each of us has lived in such a house before; at least the shape looks the same and we know before we enter that there will be twelve rooms. It's funny how we can settle in, while knowing that someday we must move.

Each year's house seems familiar from the time we set foot in it; the furnishings are, to begin with, the same. But they may change, little or much, during our tenancy. And always astonishments await us. There'll be views and vistas we didn't see from last year's house; and almost certainly a step we'd forgotten, down which we'll stumble; or a light switch which will fail, at least, temporarily.

There are certain rooms which we'll redecorate, according to our own customs, and there are rooms which will assume new contours—those of pain or mourning; and others which will be warm with joy.

Walk with me through the house of one year, all twelve rooms. It is customary to start through a door marked January, but I'd rather begin with October if you don't mind.

One fortunate thing about a year, which is bound in book covers, you can always put it aside, pick it up, and start anywhere in it, as the fancy seizes you.

Everyone's house is different except that each has the twelve rooms. Sometimes you cross a room almost too swiftly, and sometimes it's as big as all outdoors. But sooner or later you've lived in every one and then it's time to move again.

This is the house in which I lived for a year. . . .

Come in with me, the door is open.

Contents

Testament of *Trust*

October

October and I are most compatible. I was born—it seems a century or so ago—on the first day of this lovely month. To be sure, I was tardy (I've been told) by several days. This must have given me a complex because, ever since, I've always arrived too early. My dinner hostess, consequently, often greets me in curlers, or wearing an apron, or perhaps she is in the shower. You can ask Rose Franken about that; when we were neighbors and I saw her often, she was always in the bathtub when I rang her doorbell. As a girl I used to present myself for a luncheon date well before the current beau, which was not a good idea.

On October 1, 1893, I gave my mother a bad time and, I daresay, continued to do so for many years. Anyway, it seems that when I made my entrance into this world I was tossed aside, bluer than an October sky, while a famous physician worked over my mother. His assistant, discovering that I had the will to live, spanked me into shrieks. Ever since, I've had spankings one way or another, to remind me that, of all God's gifts, life is the greatest.

October is not old; she merely exhibits a delightful prime. In my section of the country the days are usually warm and the nights cool. The moon is the hunter's and while I am not happy when birds and beasties are slaughtered for man's so-called sport, I love the golden moon, round, brimming with light. Moonlight makes me melancholy; even so, I can look in wonder.

The stars seem close and, before the moon rises, very bright; and our trees have not yet lost their fire. Fading, many leaves retain a wonderful, soft color, showing toward the month's end a rosy, pale brown which is indescribable. I would give my eyeteeth—and I can't spare them—to have a suit or topcoat exactly that color, woven in a kitten-soft tweed.

October's child is supposed to be "full of woe." I've had my share—who hasn't, in whatever month they were born?—"and so," the legend continues, "life's vicissitudes must know." Whereupon we are told that to lay an opal on the October breast will counteract this difficulty—which all humans share—and hope will lull the fears to rest. I've owned numerous opals. I can't say that they gave me hope, but they certainly gave me pleasure. Hope, I've always had.

Let's walk down to the tiny pond. The afternoon sun is warm and not until the end of the month will daylight saving end. I sometimes ask myself: When we save daylight, what do we do with it?

The mallards may be on the pond, but they'll take off when they see us coming down the slope; and the cock pheasant, I hope, will crow—he sounds like a rusty gate—and take cover. On the ledge by the pond there's an old Chinese frog made of stone. He was given to me by a friend I greatly loved. All through the year he sits and stares gravely into the water, now increased by autumn rains and full of brown leaves and little willow branches.

The time for gnats, midges and mosquitoes has passed (there are reasons why I am not always pleased with summer and things which fly and buzz and sting are some of them), so we can stand here and look across the russet fields at the dark green pines and darker cedars. Somewhere a bird will be singing. . . . Let us look up at the October sky, breathe deeply, and be quiet.

I used to be so impatient; rarely with people, but always with events. When something had to be done, I didn't wait for anyone else to do it or even help; I did it myself, provided I knew how. I remember a box of books I could have waited to open and a huge basket of oranges that didn't have to be sorted for distribution right that minute. But I lifted them. . . . I'm obliged to remember because my back, even now, reminds me.

When first I moved here, I presented myself with more poison-ivy discomfort than I can tell you by tearing vines off trees and bushes or pulling plants from the ground. I was in too much of a hurry to go back to the house for shears, gloves and sprays, or to wait for a professional to tackle the job. I had to get things done, at once, that very minute! Now I have learned to slow down a little. Perhaps an illness taught me. Or perhaps it wasn't that at all because then I had no choice. I had to slow down because for a time I couldn't hurry. Actually, I think I learned by reflecting upon what is really important.

If you sit down and list the things truly vital to you, you'll be astonished how short the final inventory will be. For after you've made the first one, if you'll look at it awhile, you'll cross a few things out. Pared down to basic needs, what remains? God, love, work, shelter, your daily bread. What else is absolutely essential?

Soon the dew will fall upon the grass, the light will fade from the sky and presently the night birds will speak. It's time to go back to the house, and when we go in, let's take a crumpled yellow maple leaf or a pinkish-tan one from an oak.

This being my birthday month, I should have baked a cake. But I can't cook. In my youth, however, I could bake one kind, my favorite, which is devil's food, loaf-shaped. All I recall about the recipe is that the liquid was not milk but water. Was it boiling or merely hot? People know about this vanished art of my young womanhood—I've spoken and written about it—so they've sent me recipes from all over the country. I must now confess I've been afraid, personally, to try any of them; it is better to think nostalgically of something which was a success than to try again after a long lapse of time, and find failure; or even if my effort didn't fail cake-wise, I'm afraid what came from the oven would not taste like the devil's food I remember.

Summer's behind us now; behind us are the thunderstorms which I despise, the humidity and the long dry spells, and ahead of us the wonderful days when it's warm but not humid, and a cool wind whispers. Now I can look back to a time spent on Cape Cod—the only place I've ever been, except Hawaii and England, where I don't care what the weather's like—while I turn myself around for autumn and winter.

This turning around is literal. In the late spring the house takes to a summer dress: cool, white, green, and uncluttered; the heavy rugs up and the hooked ones down. Then, the first thing you know, it's as it is now, back in winter costume: slip covers off, and in the living room the pink curtains up and the old, deep violet rug—which was my mother's—on the floor. I like this alteration; each time the house changes over, so to speak, it seems fresh and new to me.

Perhaps that is why I can't seem to stay put in any month. My thinking is often upside down. In October I remember lilacs dripping with May rain; in December, I consider the ruby velvet of roses; and during the cold, white center of the year I find my mind walking beside a bed of valley lilies.

So, I'm a year older. I remember that when I was a child I believed that the zenith of achievement was to be grown-up. But I can't recall what, in those days, "grown-up" meant to me. I daresay I pictured someone who didn't have to go to school or be in bed at a routine time each evening, or get up when a certain hour struck next morning; in short, someone who could come, go and do as she pleased—which, I now find, is true of very few grownups.

When I advanced to eighteen, I felt older than Noah's Ark. When I was twenty-eight, I thought thirty
terrifying. I wonder why we fix upon the round numbers to worry about—why we are sure thirty-eight
isn't old but forty is. After a while forty's young and
fifty's ancient. Now sliding along in the sixties, I wonder what seventy is like?

No one really grows up, inside.

Haven't you found that true maturity is very rare?
Actually, one of the most endearing things about one's
older friends—and no matter how old you are, there's
always someone older—is their sudden graceful slipping
into a vanished childhood, through a word, or a gesture,
or an attitude. And I am not talking about senility or
memory lapses or living in the past but of the eternally
young spirit which, every now and then, looks from old
eyes and smiles.

Oh, the calendars and the mirrors, they never tell the
true story!

My month, the beginning of my personal year, always seems in between, as in a way I am. It's a long
time since spring, and summer's gone, but it isn't winter yet.

This is such a beautiful world, the small one in which
we live. Often we confuse the outside world with the
one within us and then we don't think it beautiful at
all. But the beauty of the outer world is as God created

it; men have, of course, during what is known as progress, stripped much natural loveliness from the land, and gone streaking noisily across the sky. But beauty remains; it can't all be destroyed. And on the other side of the ledger man has brought beauty to wasteland and desert.

As for the world within, in which we live more closely than the world without, that's as we ourselves make it. So when we say—and I'm guilty often enough —that we don't like this world, we are stating quite simply that we don't like ourselves.

When first I moved to this house, it stood alone, except for one other house and an old barn opposite, and the house next door to me, in which the Sisters live. Now the barn's gone and all around little country roads are being torn asunder by developments, hundreds of houses, multiple twins, mushrooming up. Just in back of this property an elementary school has recently been built and soon there won't be an inch of unoccupied land in the neighborhood except the acres next door to me and the few I call my own.

For the first time I have been plagued by people who race past in cars and toss from them much accumulated rubbish; by dogs and children chasing the pheasant, shooting arrows into bushes and firecrackers into dry fields. But people must live—and apparently without buying trash cans. And it's many a man's dream to stake out a claim to a piece of green grass and topsoil and build there. The piece may be small or large; the building a split-level, a pseudo-colonial, or personalized chicken coop; the grass plot may be the size of a man's handkerchief or eventually an impressive lawn, but it will be the dream come true, and who am I to stand— even if I could—in the way of their longings?

Secondary roads turn into first-class, and first-class expand into highways; slowly, inexorably the cities creep into suburbs and the suburbs creep into what was once rural; none can stop it, and who has the right, anyway?

While I still have trees and flowering bushes, a very small pond, and a smaller bulb garden; while I can still see pheasant skitter across a dry field, a rabbit dance in the moonlight and now and again a red fox look over a stone wall; while I still retain a space upon which to walk, I'll not really mind that the once-silent nights have become vocal and the birds disturbed. For progress is something which is for everyone and no one person for selfish interests can—or should—try to interrupt.

Occasionally I wish I'd been born even further back than I was. Say, in the 'seventies after the War between the States when there were horses and buggies, gaslights and neighbors. There were, of course, no modern appliances and gadgets to make work and living easier.

No jets flying cross country; no automobiles to get you to places faster. But with all the inconveniences which obtained, there was a certain amount of leisure. People worked longer hours and a longer week, but most of them didn't *hurry*.

This is the knife which now lacerates most of the world—the pace, the drive, the stress.

When, on a dark autumnal day, the sort of dripping, dismal day that comes in winter, with ice on the branches and treacherous mirrors of it on the roads, I think myself into my sister's rose garden, I suppose the psychiatrists would say I am trying to escape from my current surroundings. I disagree. I am just freeing and pleasuring my mind by letting it dwell on past loveliness which, God willing, will also be in the future.

Often, when old family problems increase or new ones spring up, like dandelions in May, I don't, as Gladys Taber says, know which way is from me. These are the moments when the little rodents of uncertainty and anxiety nibble at the fringes of the mind; when insecurity is as real as the floor you pace, and your pressures visibly shape you.

I read somewhere that Winston Churchill painted not to relieve tension but to create it, in times when his brilliant mind could not be employed with his country's emergencies. It is an interesting thought. And just before I read it, I saw that a doctor had said that, far from needing to discard tensions, we require them—that is the physical, not the psychological tensions—in order to accomplish whatever we have been put here to do. There is, I suppose, such a condition as being tranquilized, artificially or naturally, into something like a sofa cushion. You just sit there and are soft, amiable and comfortable. This butters no bread, however, and helps no one, least of all yourself.

Balance is a spiritual law; few of us learn to recognize, much less to obey it. Proper balance between physical tension and relaxation would create a wonderful world of happy people.

The psychological tension which, of course, reflects in the body, is due usually to a state of anxiety. The ways of overcoming it are many: the deliberate reaching up and within for quiet, the release into prayer, sometimes a counterirritation such as a physical stress.

Once, recently, in the late evening, I was greatly disturbed by an anonymous, hideous telephone call. When I had dropped the receiver back in place, I returned to the serene room in which, beside a table blooming with African violets, I'd been reading—of all things—*Plutarch's Lives*. I had all eight volumes around me, but I could no longer keep my mind on what I was reading; I kept thinking of the telephone call. I was quite aware that the caller was mentally ill, that I was only one of many victims of this sort of creeping, pitiful evil which had been literally whispered. Finally, seeing the volumes strewn about me, I decided to go downstairs and replace them on their shelves, which are the highest in the library.

Normally, it wouldn't occur to me to turn on lights, go downstairs at ten at night and wrestle with books and ladders—but I did. I moved the big table, opened up the little stepladder, replaced the books and, of course, came face to face with a disorder on those top shelves which had existed for a long time. I'd known it but ignored it, in the hope, I suppose, that it would go away.

So, I rearranged things.

It was eleven before I went back upstairs. I listened to the news and then went to bed, having forgotten, during that hour, what had so unexpectedly happened. I had not sat with a translation of Mr. Plutarch in my hands and brooded about it. I'd done something and created a physical tension which, in turn, brought about a dissipation of the psychological one.

Last spring, I think it was, over a minor upset in plans, dates and such, I went into such a stew that you could have served me for supper. My impatience again. Yet, for all concerned, everything came out beautifully, which taught me that things do work out. It wasn't the first time the lesson had been presented, but apparently

I haven't a very retentive memory. For the time being, however, I know there's no use writing, wiring, telephoning, chewing my best fingernails or screaming. A little quiet, considerable prayer, plus the practical approach which almost always includes some compromise, will eventually turn the trick—in everyone's favor.

We do borrow trouble just as we borrow other things. Most of us, at one time or another, have had to borrow money from relatives, banks or friends. One extraordinary thing about that—and I've borrowed, so I know—is the contrast it affords: the anxiety while you owe, the relief when you have the means to repay, and the downright reluctance to do so!

Borrowing trouble is something else again. There's no repayment in kind; there's not even a split second of relief; you just stay on in debt, compounding interest.

To look up and be quiet—that's the secret of true achievement in any season. Look up, look within, be still. The worries, annoyances, and fears are like the flying insects of summer, buzzing—and how loud they sound; even one mosquito in a bedroom at night seems noisier than an electric drill—stinging, and even obscuring our vision. Quietude is inside. It is trust. It is a going into the future without fear, walking from October's room into the often-dreary room of November, and past it into winter. But winter has rewards. It brings the silent snow—however much we hate to shovel it, however house-bound we become—and Christmas.

Once it's Christmas, the year turns, and we look toward spring.

For the young, the wheel of the seasons turns slowly; for the older, so quickly we grow dizzy with it, as one season whirls into the next.

If the years have taught me anything, it is to trust; no matter how disturbed the surface of the river we call life may be, beneath is the stillness, the deep water, the calm.

So I wish you many happy returns of my birthday. There have been so many; I don't know how many more there will be, and do not, truly, care. I love this world and all its beauty. I know that in many of its manifestations there is ugliness—in what people do, in the way millions must live, in the attitudes man expresses, which influence the world. But I am happy to be in the world now, privileged to live in it, to take what comes while learning to accept, and to look ahead.

As one room leads into another, so does one month into the next. There is always a future, there is always hope.

When as tonight, now that dark has fallen, we look to a moon-flooded sky and hear leaves loosening from the branches or obstinately rustling as they cling, we experience, I think, however dimly, a universal grasp of truth: that wherever we are, no matter what our circumstances, our security lies in love, earthly and divine, and in quietude and trust.

Threshold

Everybody knows that between two rooms, or a hallway and a room, there's something called a threshold. I just looked the word up in the Oxford Dictionary and wish I hadn't, because I'm considerably confused. Apparently it means, first, "the piece of timber wood or stone below the bottom of a door, which must be crossed in entering a house"; it's also "the sill of a doorway, an entrance to a house or building." However, it appears to be "the upper horizontal part of a doorcase," and likewise, "figuratively the border or limit, the line which one crosses in entering." Way back in 1586, which even I don't remember, it was used in reference to "entrance, the beginning of a state, or action. . . ."

I've never been a purist (though my father was), so if no one minds, I'll use the threshold to cross from one month to another, from one room in the year's house to the next.

According to the calendar, there's no threshold between October and November, no sharp dividing line in time; whether you happen to be up—or asleep—on October thirty-first when the clock strikes midnight—well, it's November.

But I'd rather pause a moment between the two rooms, and call the pause a threshold. You know how it is when you leave a room familiar to you and go into the next; you experience a small hesitancy, for you aren't quite sure what's over the sill.

The word "threshold" has been used in many ways since it was first invented; doctors often speak about the threshold of pain, for instance; and psychologists of the threshold of attention; some, it seems, are low, and some are high. I've found that I have a threshold, too— my way to being quiet, and alone, and to something which, for lack of a better word, I call "meditation."

It's not, of course, in the accepted sense. I do not assume unusual postures or look fixedly at an object, whether a rose or a crystal ball, or seek to clear my mind of its all-day clutter and rubbish. I can't, that's why. So I simply say my own sort of prayers and usually aloud, for there's no one present in the flesh to hear me and my life has been one of words, written and spoken.

I am not at all concerned with how anyone prays or meditates or performs what is called "going into the silence." To each, the way that is best, simplest and most rewarding for him. What is orthodox to one, is unorthodox to another. I do not believe it matters whether you repeat prayers by rote, turn a wheel, endeavor to withdraw yourself from ordinary consciousness, or simply say aloud what you feel and think. For whatever you do or don't do, think, say, or don't say, I am certain that God understands.

In my everyday life (and all life is everyday, isn't it? As a dear friend of mine once remarked, the trouble with life is it's so *daily*), I cross my own threshold each night from anxiety and business, work and play, into a room of quiet and reflection, confession and seeking. It can be at midnight, it can be earlier or later, but there hasn't been a night in years (saving only those in which I was ill and, for all practical purposes, unconscious or incompetent) that I haven't taken a little time out between darkness and the dim, oncoming dawn to think back and to look ahead, to search, to ask and to promise to submit.

It's not a bad idea to cross the threshold from one room of the year, one month, to another in such a fashion. We now know all that outwardly happened to us in October, and, dimly, something of what happened inwardly as well. We know what we have to carry forward with us and what we must regretfully, or happily, as the case may be, leave behind.

We don't know what's in the room called November. Oh, our engagement pads will list any number of things we seem required or feel we want to do; but these are only pencil scrawls on pieces of paper. We know that there will be a day set aside called Thanksgiving. But what more do we know?

Cross, then, the threshold. Having pondered somewhat and prayed, having left behind the outworn or futile things, take those which will be useful to you across the threshold—into the room called November.

November

November is the month of delicately faded leaves—mauve, brown and pink—and of birds, halting brightly and briefly at the feeders to say hello or good-bye. It is also Thanksgiving time, which everyone knows shouldn't be just for one day. This has been written in books, set down in newsprint and preached from pulpits and lecterns for years; usually without avail.

This is also, at its beginning, the month of local or national elections. It's an ending of one period, the start of another, and a month in which you can, in my part of the world, expect snow or Indian summer, or both.

At this season, I hang colored corn at the doorway and put unadorned twin pumpkins on either side of the worn old stone steps. For some years I've used gourds in the living room and hallway, usually in a pale gray-green Sung bowl. Gourds are lovely in contour and color—yellow, orange, green, striped. They fade out with time and weigh no more than feathers. I like them and generally keep them until the spring. There are dried flowers about the house, too: a tiny arrangement in an egg cup which my son and his wife gave me; a framed posy of Australian flowers; and many bowls filled with seemingly everlasting bright yellows, purples, off-whites and soft rose.

This year I had to discard at last the dried hydrangeas I brought from the Cape long ago; they'd faded from blue into mauve, green, aquamarine and brown, then settled into an ineffable sort of beige and become so fragile that, if I simply walked by, a petal detached itself and fell silently to the floor. Also I've had to dispose of the bayberries, which for years I had in the Chinese wall vases. I suppose they grew tired of being at the foot of the stairs, for one night as I went by the branches quietly loosed their hold on the berries and showered them all over me and the floor.

Now I have sprays of silvery white honesty, and stalks of dark brown cattails and, in each hanging vase, one great gray leaf, the name of which I do not know; and in the old, very large luster mug which my sister gave me I have little branches of pine from just outside the door.

Now is the time to delve into the gift chest in the study and haul out things I bought last summer and put away. Some of these completely astonish me. For whom did I buy them and why?

This is the season, also, to start wrapping next month's presents. I regret to say that unless I remember to put things in the gift chest I lose them. And sometimes when I wrap things, I either lose or forget the card or tag, and have to undo the packages just before Christmas. I'll never get over my habit of retracing steps.

Now is the period of addressing Christmas cards. Perhaps like me, you start in October, but I wonder if you have the address-book trouble I do. I can't read my own writing, and I scribble between lines, on margins and sideways. Some names have question marks after them. Why? Some are crossed off. Every so often, laboriously, and a few pages at a time, I do over my book. It starts out just fine, in pencil, so that I can erase and put in a new address, since nowadays people appear to move every year or so, but by the time I've reached the Z's—and I know a couple of Z people—it's a hopeless maze.

After some names there are cryptic notations, most of which appear to refer to food, so I must have had these people here for dinner. A generation ago you never thought of your guests' allergies; maybe they didn't have them or didn't know it if they did. I don't suppose the word had been invented. Or perhaps a lot of people had fathers like mine. He made me eat everything, because, he said, "I will *not* have a child who will grow up to embarrass a hostess!"

So I ate everything, no matter how much my eyes swelled afterwards. (I was, it later appeared, allergic to clams.)

You'd be surprised at the list I've made of "allergies" —from fried foods (usually the ulcer people) to shell- or any kind of fish; even to vinegar, cream sauces, liver and cheese. In any case, having asked, "Will you come to dinner (for the first time) next week?" I further inquire "Have you dislikes or allergies?" and then write them down.

Heaven be praised Thanksgiving dinner rarely upsets anyone unless they eat too much. And those who hate boiled onions, squash or yellow turnips needn't eat them. Most folks can tolerate turkey, mashed or sweet potatoes and cranberry sauce and can refuse pie.

Have you noticed how Thanksgiving has come to mean a big meal? Originally, on that day people had a special dinner and gave thanks; it was a time for friends and relatives to gather together, but nowadays a great many people think of it simply as a day on which you just feast, and most of them, especially those in city apartments no longer bother to cook. They go out. So do I now, for Gussie, who cooks for me, has that day at home. I take my daughter and her children to a quiet, uncrowded place where they serve turkey and the trimmings, too. If you go to the others, they are, from noon on, so crammed with children and adults you are bound to get the idea that Thanksgiving is merely the day when overeating is protocol.

As I said earlier, we've been told for a long time that giving thanks one day a year isn't enough; for, today, tomorrow, yesterday, and every day as long as you live, there's usually something to be grateful for—the shape of a cloud, or a bending tree, sunny weather, or needed rain; a telephone call from a child living away from home or a friend you thought had forgotten you; a letter from parent, lover, friend; the unexpected gift, the hoped-for success—all the good things which happened a while ago, all the things we can look forward to.

The other day someone said to a group of us, "Never forget, each day you live to be grateful. There's so little real gratitude in the world, not only toward those about you but to the God within you."

Looking back over a comparatively long and often

stormy life, I can see objectively how it has been balanced, the good and bad, the easy times and the hard. I
sometimes tell myself that I'm put upon, that I've had
more than my share of disaster. But it isn't so. I've had
exactly the trouble I was supposed to have (having
brought some of it upon myself) and an equal share of
happiness.

It's a far cry to the Pilgrims, maize, wild turkey and
Indians, but I'm certain that, when the first Thanksgiving took place, it really was to give thanks. . . . Oh I
know that in this day and age people around countless
tables in this country look to those who sit at the head
and say grace. How many really listen?

Grace is not merely something committed to memory and uttered aloud before soup is served or the
knife slices into the crisp brown skin of the All-Ameri-
can bird. Grace is a living thing. "Saving grace," they
say from the pulpits. It's a phrase flexibly used, and in
ordinary ways of life: "There but for the grace of
God, go I." Or, in idle conversation, how often do you
hear someone say, "Her saving grace is her sense of
humor"?

And it could be so, for a true sense of humor is, I
think, a sense of proportion, and in some—a few fortunate people—I have found that humor extends itself
to a sort of gentle gaiety.

I daresay each person's saving grace is different,

something which illuminates him, and makes him a little special. It could be the ability to see the other side of a situation, or a greater ability which is wholeheartedly to love. And certainly it could be true humility of mind and spirit. . . . Whatever my saving grace or yours, I hope it will be brighter and more enduring than the candles which light a festive meal.

I just turned from the typewriter to answer the telephone and then walked into the living room to look for something. It has started to snow just a little, very quietly. This is a fine snow and not as lazy as some, as it appears to be driving along in a purposeful direction. There's a cardinal sitting in the branches of the mulberry tree. He does not look discouraged.

As I went by the bowl with the dried yellow flowers in it, I remembered stopping to buy them at a wayside stand a little over a year ago, when a friend was driving me home from a visit upstate. They have stayed as gay and fresh as when I bought them. Perhaps they are somewhat dusty—it's a perilous job, dusting dried flowers, so, usually you don't—but I wish I could capture their eternal-seeming freshness.

Now that the house is back to winter, I like it better than ever. (I also say this when it turns back to summer.) The little hall has a particular charm. The Copenhagen figures on the table are sleepy bears—one a cub—and a dormouse, and I usually put white and red, or yellow and bronze flowers there, so when you enter there is a feeling of warmth.

I hesitate to confess that we rarely use our fireplaces because we do not need them for warmth except when there's furnace trouble, which, I have noticed, usually occurs on the coldest days of winter and always on a Saturday or Sunday.

However, the fireplaces are not neglected, and sometimes we build a fire and light it just for looks. In summer I put white-birch logs on the living-room hearth and a huge white shell outside the fire screen. In winter there are giant cones, sent me by a friend from Nevada. And there's a built-in woodbox under the nearest window so, if a fire's needed, we have the makings.

Here and there, the house needs touching up. Isn't it extraordinary how the plaster in an old house cracks right after redoing or the wallpaper starts to curl? I often sit alone of an evening and think hopelessly of the paint jobs to be done. I think: But it was *just* done, only a couple of years ago. And then I remember, with horror, that the living room and library were last repainted in late '54, the dining room and a guest room in about '56, and somewhere along in there my own room was repapered and perhaps another. . . .

Mercy, the whole house should be done over! But

where I am to hide during that process? Or how finance it?

It is perhaps even more startling to think of the house in which the spirit resides.

This is the house of flesh of which St. Paul wrote, in which the human spirit lives from the hour of its birth into this world until its departure. And the house shows wear. We are all acquainted with the outward signs, the creaking joints, the lesser agility, the tendency to slump and show widening cracks of fatigue.

Now and then, I take a long hard look at my personal house and am the better for it, albeit chastened. How cramped the human spirit must feel! Oh, there are lots of rooms, no doubt, but what kind and how furnished? Do doors stand open to friend and stranger, or are they locked and barred? And whose brain is not an attic full of old trunks and other discarded luggage, or else a basement crowded with the unwanted?

Occasionally I force myself to try and clean my personal attic just as I have the one in this wooden house cleaned. When I go up there alone, I find more and more things I can give or throw away. But the attic of the mind seems to need a continual turning-out.

Some time ago I was critically ill and, as I got better, I found myself compelled to do some cleaning. I had long since tossed out dusty envies and jealousies and tried to get rid of regrets—but some of them kept coming back, like bats. And then I discovered, in a small locked case a couple of resentments. They'd been there a long time. I got rid of them by the only method I knew, which was to admit them to the people concerned, and apologize. I've no doubt they thought I was crazy, but the attic seems cleaner.

There's just no use in storing up the futilities, trivialities and prejudices. I suspect that the spirit often walks in attic or basement and must feel considerable discouragement. So the least we can do for the immortal spark which dwells within each of us is to offer it as decent a habitation as possible and as much sun and space and air as we can manage. That's not easy; you have to knock out barriers and partitions.

Even newly built houses are furnished with much which would be better discarded. Older ones show symptoms of dilapidation. Well, there's always a new idea, a useful job, to brighten things up like a coat of fresh paint.

We see the visible world about us, wide or narrow, according to our environment and to our reaches of vision. A far-reaching vision can go a million miles past any environment. I have known people living in wretched circumstances who, through imagination, have seen more of the world than I. But the invisible world in which we live is that of ourselves; and vision is necessary, windows for the mind and windows for the spirit.

The night has fallen now, and the rising wind is talking to me in the chimneys. In all this house the only light is the one above my typewriter. I could, of course, get up and turn on others. I have bruised more shins, stubbed more toes and howled more recriminations at inanimate objects than I can count, because I'm too lazy, or too interested in what I'm doing, to get up from my chair and touch a few switches. But I hope that the place in which my spirit lives always affords some light, even in the dark corners where sorrow and tragedy—which are almost bound to seek out everyone at one time or another—lie like heaps of clotted dust. They are awfully hard to sweep out; perhaps we never succeed, but, we can always try.

I'll get up and put on the lights over the outside door, so they shine on the ears of Indian corn and the bright woolen strands of yarn which suspend them. It will not be long now before I take these down and put in their place old sleigh bells on a leather strap.

Back at my desk I shall answer a letter I had the other day from a friend who bade me count my blessings (I must have been complaining to her). I shall tell her that of course I count them—children and friends, love and understanding, shelter and bread and anything which has been accomplished, however little. Perhaps I should include the house in which the spirit lives, grateful that it has been strong enough to withstand storm and gale and disaster.

A thankful heart is, at this, or any season, a saving grace. So I am grateful to you for visiting with me and I wish you a Thanksgiving of body, mind and spirit better than any you've ever had so far.

Corridor

Now, if it's all right with you, I'll build a little path between November and December. We know there isn't one, but in a book you can do anything. So I'll stop the clocks and turn the calendar to the wall.

Our recent snowfall lasted no time at all; after it, we had rain, which froze; then the sun came out, the ice melted and it was autumn again, seemingly nowhere near winter. I think of the cold weather ahead with some trepidation. I love to look out at winter from inside; I don't mind going outdoors—when the snow is heaped and fresh and clean—to about as far as the feeder. I'm scared to death to drive in it most of the time, or rather, to be driven. I just sit, a quiet passenger. Then, too, there's always trouble with trains, which arrive late or not at all, and the business of calling up people, or being called by them, when suddenly you can't get anywhere because of road conditions.

If I have to walk down a brick path—and if I'm to leave this house at all, it has to be by a brick path or through the yard—and see as much as a pinpoint of ice, I fall down, in my mind.

I wonder what the pioneer people did?

All in all, I would have made a very poor showing as a pioneer. I once learned how to clean oil lamps, but that was a long time ago at a camp on the river. And Gladys Taber taught me how, properly, to build a fire. She can cook; and in a fireplace, too. As for me, I approach even a gas or electric range with fear and trembling, and my few experiences with ovens have been horrifying. But armed with all the new appliances, I could keep myself going through storms, now that I have a generator—and plenty of canned goods as well.

I'm afraid the pioneer women had more to do than that. My brain reels when I think of it all—the carrying of water, the scratching a garden from stony soil, the stoking of fires, the meals . . . and, for heaven's sake, the washing up. To say nothing of bears, Indians, snakes, or whatever threatened.

When you think of the fortitude of the men and women who fought the wildernesses of this country and of others before America was discovered; when you pause to imagine what they endured in hostility, terror and disease, in grief, determination and the courage of desperation, don't you feel ant-small? . . . No? . . . I do.

All of us have pioneer blood, whether we were born in this or some other country. There have always been frontiers, both geographical and of the mind, to challenge men, and there are always uncharted stretches of the spirit, where we are, each of us, pioneering, facing hostilities, making pacts and compromises almost every day of our lives.

In these individual dominions there is much to overcome; there is always ground to clear and plough, and weeds to pull, once the seeds are sown. We clear a little patch, turn our backs for a moment, and the jungle creeps up, the poisonous vines encroach; the wilderness, repelled, has again advanced. Or a wind blows from some unknown quarter and what we had thought fallow ground lies buried under a blanket of sterile sand.

What we must realize is that we have been given weapons, tools, which are of the spirit; these are basic, and of tempered steel; the axe with which to cut through prejudice; the machete of determination which slashes into a wilderness of indecision, and above all the shield of faith, of conviction in the justice and compassion and mercy of God.

And the thoughts I have set down here are just a passageway to next month; a way in which we are, for the moment, walking—toward December.

December

Long before the Christmas season wreaths hang at the doors and the sleigh bells wait a hand to stir them into life. A week, or more, before the Eve itself I start to dress the house for the season. If you come in, you will find it untidy, full of boxes packed with ornaments and angels; you can peer into the gift chest at the wrapped packages, and at those yet to be wrapped. Because, by early December, the last package which must be mailed has gone and in the chest there are only family things or those which I deliver in person.

Everywhere, the old adornments and the angels. Each year when the cartons are brought down from the attic, I unpack them and find something I'd forgotten. It's such fun and so satisfying, though a forgotten angel has often regarded me with reproach.

This is a smaller house than the one which I once made holly bright; the tree is smaller and there are fewer people around the dining-room table on Christmas Eve and Christmas Day, but it's still Christmas and would be were I alone and in a one-room dwelling.

I am so sorry for those who consider Christmas a chore. Of course, most of us knock ourselves out, yet some of us enjoy it. The people who rush from shop to shop consulting reluctant lists and fervently wishing that it were all over, and spring at hand, have my sympathy.

I admit preparations are physically tiring; everyone knows that, because no matter how well prepared you think you are—I bought Christmas presents in Nova Scotia in July—you're never quite caught up.

I am saddened for, and by, the people who excuse their lack of valid interest, or admit only to a mere conforming to custom, by harping on the commercial aspect of the season. There is a commercial aspect to all seasons, whether or not festivals occur within them. Merchants must live, and through employment, help others to do so. But the commercialism need not be in an individual heart; just in the shop windows, the advertising, the neon lights.

This is the season of the caller, of people I haven't seen for a year or more because they live too far away, or are too busy to come, or think I am too busy to see them. But at this time, no one feels like an intruder, and none is unwelcome.

Among my callers are my many non-Christian friends, who love the warmth and gentle gaiety, and sense the spirit of the season. Hanukkah, the Festival of Lights has often coincided, calendar-wise with Christmas; and in India at this time lights are in every home, for another, but still festive and holy season.

Now the packages have begun to arrive from faraway places and are sitting on the top of the chest, a most unhandy spot because, when I want to open it, I'll have to take them off; eventually they'll all end up on the floor.

Holiday gifts are such fun to give and to accept! But there are also the daily gifts for which we do not write thank you notes. For these I am increasingly grateful, in true humility and in pride, which is humility's sister. I don't mean vanity.

For the humble spirit accomplishes what would be impossible to the body: although upon its knees, it walks upright.

People to whom a gift is just something, useful or

not, which someone has bought and sent—usually someone to whom they feel they must send a gift in turn—have my compassion. I've had some I can't imagine anyone employing for any purpose, and these I regard, as the King of Siam reportedly said, with puzzlement; but also with respect.

I may not be able to use the hand-painted doily, the woven what-is-it, or the carved gimmick, but maybe somebody can, and anyway the gift is not the doily, the straw, or the shaped wood but the evidence that someone thought of me.

No one can really make Christmas commercial for you—not the merchants (who, as I said, must earn a living) nor your harried, wish-it-were-over friends; nor even the witty, the cynical and dissatisfied. You alone have that power.

A child does not stop to ponder on trade mark-ups and gross income when he looks at the bright red wagon under the tree. He doesn't consider whence it came or through how many hands—and items in account books—it has passed. He is not affronted by the loud blaring of radios and record players which smite the crisp air with carols, starting in November. He is not disturbed by garishness of any shop or street. He thinks only of the red wagon on Christmas morning. Being a child, he gives little thought to the person who gave it to him, whether it's Santa Claus or a parent. It is a red wagon. It is his—this treasure. He may break it tomorrow, forget it next day or tire of it next week. But the moment of discovery is his moment; a moment of wonder.

The adult, if he is fortunate, has retained within himself enough of the child to experience the wonder, no matter how often in a lifetime it's been repeated. Well, not exactly repeated; each wonder differs somewhat from another. And the adult, if he has a loving heart, thinks also of him who sent what approximates the child's red wagon.

When I fill a stocking for a distant, grown-up child or one who lives nearby, I am as full of rejoicing as the stocking is of small packages. Most of them contain eminently practical things. I never had a daughter, close by or away, who didn't hate to spend money on cold cream, shampoo, hair nets, nail files, tooth pastes . . . the list goes on and on. One once said to me unhappily that for the first time in her life she had been forced to buy a new lipstick. Seems I'd forgotten to put one in her stocking.

Don't think I haven't a stocking. It is extremely large, and knitted, so it stretches. It was given me by a friend. It has my name on it, a date, and various knitted-in decorations, Christmas trees and the like. It scorns sequins. Quite a while before Christmas I hang it, mutely, upon the fireplace screen and wait for it to vanish. It always does. The nearby child fills it, and other children and friends send contributions to her.

On Christmas morning, very early, I sneak downstairs, alone, and take it back to bed with me and before I've made coffee or roused anyone else in the house, I sit there and open up the packages filled with delicacies, idiocies and charm—no child of mine gives me anything practical—and am as excited as though I were seven years old with all eternity before me.

That's a misleading sentence—for while I'm not seven, still, all eternity's before me.

Speaking of eternity, I always wonder what happens to time? When, nowadays, the cartons come down from the attic, I can't believe it, for surely it was only last week or, at the remotest, last month that the Christmas things were packed away and all but two of the angels folded their docile wings to dream, in banishment, for a year.

The two which remain downstairs are fragile and so they are kept in sight: the tall one, in her delicate colors, in the upper hall; the pure, white, praying cherubim in my bedroom.

Well, everyone knows that as we grow older, time collapses upon itself, folding back like the inside shutters in the living room. Yesterday was Christmas. Tomorrow will be.

My parents had Christmas hearts and their own customs. Over the years those I first knew remain with me and others have been added; my children will remember their earlier Christmases, as I do mine.

I like to think of family customs; and like most people I am proud of family achievement, but only recently have I thought of the pride we are all entitled to feel in our common origin.

My own ancestors were, for the most part, clergymen, governors, editors, teachers, lawyers, missionaries or medical men; they fought their battles in peace and in war; they built with their hands and dreamed with their hearts and spoke out their minds. They were hardworking people. There's a certain pride in looking back. But it hasn't anything to do with yourself; you weren't the teacher, preacher, editor; these achievements aren't yours.

Every human being, however, can take pride in his kinship to the Creator. For in this we are truly brothers and it has nothing to do with creeds, customs, environments, countries, or pigmentations of the skin.

We talk so much about brotherhood and so rarely contemplate the unalterable fact that there is one God, no matter in what way we worship Him, and that all are created by, belong to, and return to, Him and are, therefore, brothers.

Earth law, as we all know, is not always justice. But spiritual law is balance, and balance is justice and justice is love. Spiritual law offers us a golden coin: on one side, humility; on the other, pride.

To be able to walk our separate roads in happy humility and joyous pride is something which we all have to work to achieve—and understand.

I have spent some strange Christmases: two in Germany during the First World War; one in a semitropical country where it was hard for me to think of pines, as I looked at palms; one in our north where the snow continually fell and the air was as sweet and cold as ice cream. And I remember, even though I try to forget, a Christmas which—despite the lights and tree, packages, ornaments and wreaths to which I stubbornly clung— was more dreadful than nightmare. And still another for which I flew home from London just in time to trim the house, the living-room tree, the birds' tree on the terrace, and celebrate with the children and friends I hadn't seen for three months. After which I ignominiously took to my bed with one of the alleged viruses.

The only hurting thing nowadays about Christmas, as far as I am concerned, is the knowledge that there are children who wake to an empty day, and old people huddled away with none to remember them; and hospital wards in which, although students sing carols and there is turkey for dinner and a tree and packages from certain committees, there is loneliness, pain and remembering; nothing of one's own really; and no one to whom to give if one had anything.

I often want to ask the people who say that Christmas wearies them: Have you ever thought how terrible it would be if there were no one to whom you could give?

At Christmas, beneath the enchanting wrappings there is the sharing. She who creates bright jellies in her kitchen, dresses them in red and green paper and ties them with ribbon, has shared more than the woman who is able to go to a great store and send a gift with a casual card.

We can't all make jellies—I can't for one—and we can't all command the charming extravagances of the shops, but we can share. Anyone who believes in the spirit of Christmas—this has now become, of course, a cliché, but clichés are often truisms and the Spirit of Christmas is true—believes in the underlying sharing, a quiet beauty, and so is happy. But the forlorn children, the forgotten old, the neglected, need reassurance, the knowledge of being loved.

A few of the very old may have had that knowledge —the neglected child has not. But I have seen in almost sightless eyes, vision, and in a groping hand, strength. Such a person, however anonymous, alone or forgotten, knows he is loved, despite outward appearances, and by Whom.

Lay aside the pressures, forget the budget, dismiss from your mind—don't let it give you *all* the orders—the second cousin in Wisconsin who sent you something but wasn't on your list. Ignore the fact that your feet do hurt and maybe your head aches, too, and you haven't the slightest idea how you'll get through the next few days. You'll get through them. You always have, haven't you? And if an image of your own personal little red wagon remains—and I hope it does—you'll wake refreshed on Christmas morning, with the old excitement, the inborn feeling of marvel, and come downstairs, or go into the next room, look at your tree and your stocking and thank God, your spirit kneeling.

That's Christmas.

Everything's a gift—the cards (which we take for granted), the telephone call we never dreamed would come, the letter from far places, the little blossoming plant from someone we had not heard from in years; and, perhaps, particularly the smile exchanged between strangers on a crowded street.

In God's calendar there are many holidays, no matter when they fall in the Georgian way of counting. I would celebrate them all in my heart, I would share in everything which is sacred to any man. For it is only through an accident of birth that I am here and what I am.

So come in, rest your feet and lift your heart. Take off your shoes if that will help; perhaps tea will dispel the ache above your brows. The sleigh bells at the door ring in the wind, and the wreaths—will they be flecked with white by the twenty-fourth? Look at the angels flying silently about the room; light, if you wish, the pine cones in the fireplace, and remember that all through the year there is warmth on the hearthstone of the heart, whatever the season.

Could you use the hand-painted doily? . . . I thought not. Never mind, here are cookies from overseas. Gussie has not made ours as yet, nor have the Sisters next door, who always bring us dozens in a bright tin box. What are you looking forward to? There must be something. My back hurts, and I've broken three fingernails. But presently there will be a scent of pine and I shall find carols on the radio and trim the tree. The little old angels will spread their wings wider and on Christmas Eve my children's children will stumble off to bed.

I am grateful for this—and every season. On much of this country snow will fall, if not on desert and oasis, and the south land. It won't fall Down Under; it's summer there. The earth revolves and the seasons differ, as far as weather is concerned, but that which is of the heart is unchanged, world 'round.

And world 'round, men pray for peace.

Pray with me, sharing this moment as a part of my family, and wherever and whoever you are, and in any weather, a blessed Christmas.

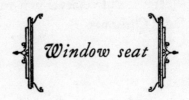

Window seat

This time, between the months, I'll build a window seat—figuratively, of course; I can't put two and two together, much less pieces of wood.

I like window seats, having lived in several houses which possessed them. They are fine places to curl up in, if you're a child of curlable size, particularly if your mother has provided cushions. Some of these old-fashioned nooks had draperies you could pull together, so you could sit there behind the curtains, in a charming privacy with a book and an apple, and, when you felt like it, look out of the windows.

In the house I had before this one, my study was a species of sun porch and beneath all the casement windows there were seats. I keep trying to remember if they opened, for storage. As I have told you, the only one in this house does open, for small logs and kindling.

I think I'll build this window seat to open, so we can store away the things we want to keep safely: memories, reflections, completed assignments, the echo of an unsolicited word of praise or encouragement. I doubt if a month passes during which someone hasn't said an encouraging word.

The window seat in the corridor between the months should afford us a view. The look backward into December, still very clear and detailed, and a look forward, into January. That's a little misty, but we can see what we hope to accomplish, what we know we must do, and what we wish would happen—if anything ever "happens." I don't think it does. I am not a fatalist. I simply believe that almost everything, whether for better or worse, is a springing up of seeds which have been planted—usually, although not always, by ourselves.

So close the top of the window seat on the intangible you want left there—and, let's go!

January

Now that the calendar New Year has arrived I suppose I should open my door although the years do not need such service; any year opens many doors for us.

I have a new desk calendar . . . all those pages . . . it seems incredible that they should fill up with names, times, reminders. But they will. Gradually, as I tear off the sheet of a day completed, the bulk of the calendar will diminish and, first thing I know, I'll be saying frantically, "Please, will someone stop and buy me an engagement pad. It's only December, but I've promised to do this or that in January!"

We have so long been portraying the new year as a baby—male at that; can't it ever be a girl?—ringing bells or rattles, and standing around, practically mother-naked, in the snow, starting itself off, as it were, with pneumonia. And the poor old year, tottering off on a crutch, and sporting a long gray beard. I've never seen a year-old child with a long gray beard, but anything can happen in, and to, a year—and usually does.

I rather like the idea of the new year sauntering in—not creeping or toddling—at the door of everyone's house, but it's even better to think of it as a house in itself; swept and garnished, the floors and furniture polished; all the clutter tossed out, and everywhere, for welcome, flowers. I'd have a fireplace, too, and a warm flame burning upward.

I wish we could make it so; ending each year with a cleaning away of all the fears, anxieties and miseries which the past twelve months may have brought, and retaining only the lovely, happy, quiet things. It would be difficult, for who among us does not carry over into the morning the worries of the day before, and into a new year the accumulations of the old?

Looking back, as we all do, it appears that the year just past had its shares of alarms and excursions; the gloomy headlines, the publicly expressed jitters, the rise of some new, unpleasant factor, the decline of things we'd like to see rise; and of course, disaster, brought about by nature—the nature of the world around us, and man's nature.

My own year had its quota of ups and downs. One of my failings is to accept the ups as a matter of course, and even wonder, like a child on a swing which doesn't go high enough, why they aren't up-er—and then to scream and start tearing my whitening locks when the swing starts downward. That's when I complain there's no end to the down.

Actually, if we took an objective look at any bygone twelve months, we'd find a balance struck; for every loss there is, somewhere, gain; for grief, a joy; and for fear, new hope. It is normal to feel the loss more acutely than the gain, and the grief more poignantly than the joy. But somehow the accounts come out even if you take into consideration not only the twelve months just past but all those which have, in your lifetime, gone before.

It's the unexpected which throws us. Usually we can make some preparation for the storm we see coming— as we do in the house when the dark clouds close in, and the wind rises. Even before the first heavy drop of rain, the first bright slash of lightning, the initial announcement of thunder, we can close windows, making things as secure as possible until the storm is over.

But sometimes one hits so suddenly there just isn't time.

Last summer, Gladys Taber wrote me that out of a clear sky a wind arose; the windows by her desk were open and before she could cross the room, a cherished old mug and a moss-rose bone dish which had been quietly sitting on the desk, minding their own business, were swept to the floor and smashed into shards.

Mugs and bone dishes may not be irreplaceable, but every now and then a high wind screams in from an unknown quarter and something we have treasured is damaged beyond repair.

I can formulate no philosophy with which to combat shock. I've tried to cushion myself against fear, but when the wholly unforeseen arises, there's no cushion. About the only thing any of us can do, I suppose, after the tears are shed and the hands wrung, is to sweep up the pieces and go on. Oh, I know hundreds of books have been written telling us "How To . . ." Among them, how to insulate ourselves against anything unpleasant, material or emotional, but as far as I'm concerned the final remedy is a very old one. When the pieces are too splintered to put together, the shock too great to permit planning or thinking, or the new burden heavier than any you have been carrying or have ever known before, you don't try to do anything yourself. You put it in God's hands.

The new year is never something cut from bright,

new cloth; it's another piece of the pattern, and woven into it is all which was in the old year; personally, for each of us; universally for the world in which we live. The fears the world has experienced for so long, go on; graphs and statistics rise and fall; the community, national and world problems as of December thirty-first, still exist; you can't simply cut the old year off like a branch and cast it away. The tree remains. There'll be new branches and always the old structure of roots and trunk, the origins of every branch.

To each of us in this year will come, I hope, happiness, lovely astonishments and going forward in our individual life; and to many of us there will come shocks and disappointments, worries, tensions and sorrows. In the world men will go on making efforts to establish peace, to decrease crime and violence; to lessen want and to help through dedicated organizations, the sick and hungry, the widow and the fatherless. Science will show many new developments, all begun last year, or long before last year. I do most earnestly feel that yesterday's dream may become tomorrow's reality; yesterday's faint hope, tomorrow's conviction; yesterday's vision, tomorrow's certainty.

People keep saying that, despite all progress, the world—do they mean its people?—regresses. The record doesn't bear this out; for the record, the world goes forward however slowly and painfully. And so do we.

I have long thought, and often said, that for every few steps I took, I went back one. This was dismal until I realized I was still a step or two ahead. In order to climb a mountain you have to start at the bottom; if there were no depths, the heights would not exist.

I don't make resolutions. An annual resolve, which seldom is kept anyway, seems to me inadequate—as if we made a policy of saying our prayers on alternate Tuesdays. Resolutions, in the plural, are for every day, as is resolution, in the singular. And every day is for hope.

If I were to "resolve" anything—and you can read another meaning into that word; the English language is very flexible—I would try to resolve my problems, and then resolve, in the New Year sense, not to have accidents. I appear to be minor-accident prone. I am sure that many mishaps are unavoidable, but not mine. No one has stubbed more toes, run into things in the dark, stepped on as many sharp stones or turned more ankles than I. I'm always hurting myself in a mild sort of way, and then asking myself pitifully: Why? So, this year, I am determined to watch where I'm going; not to fall down steps, or up, either (I've done that, too); not to dash out of bed without turning on a light, thus encountering a bookcase where it shouldn't be, or the sly, reaching-out rocker; and not to skid on the book or magazine I've dropped on the floor and permitted to remain there. I shall make a really noble endeavor to walk with certainty, to turn on the light or—if light's already there, natural or manufactured—to watch where I'm going.

This only means I shall try not to be so impatient.

Impatience is destructive. I've had to cancel many plans because I was in such a hurry to make them I didn't consider routes, time, or even other people. I've mailed dozens of letters I need not have written, simply because the first one, written the very instant I thought of it, had to be explained, apologized for, amplified or changed.

Over and over, the lesson has been given to me: slow up, reflect, look where you're going. But I haven't learned it, yet. . . .

Perhaps, this year?

One thing I have learned in recent months is how to be ill. Not seriously—because when you're seriously ill you can't hurry anything, and are often so turned inward upon yourself that you feel little concern for the world outside. But in a time or two of illness which was annoying rather than serious, I found I could wait to be well again, knowing I would be. I learned to trust in the healing available to me, in the wisdom of physicians who had spent many years learning how to heal, in the silent work of nature herself and in the healing which comes from one's own spirit, which is part of

God. So for almost the first time in my life I was in no hurry to get up, rush to the desk, remake the broken appointments, or to catch up with the mail and everyday living. I waited, and was grateful and almost content and presently everyone was congratulating me on my remarkable powers of recuperation—and no relapses.

Every day is, or can be—a recuperation from those illnesses which aren't physical: yesterday's attitudes which influence today, and today's anxieties which darken tomorrow. We attach a great deal of significance to the big dramatic events of our lives and too little to ordinary, daily living, to what we think and say and do.

Let's take a vow. I still don't mean to make a resolution. Most of us, if we take a vow, regard it seriously; at least we intend to keep our promises, which is more than we can say of the usual resolutions. Let us therefore vow to keep on going and, when we slide back a step or two, not to sit down and stay there but to get up and advance again. Vows, I am sure, reward us according to the measure of our effort and sincerity.

No one can alter himself overnight. The man-made miracles of science did not occur in the time it takes to say "Thomas Edison." The great discoveries, in any field of endeavor, did not happen from one moment to the next. They didn't happen at all, really. Perhaps, in one illuminated moment, the last piece of a puzzle fell into place, but back of the completed picture were the years of patient, painstaking work, of disappointment and failure, and of trying again.

Nature, however suddenly she presents us with her storms and earthquakes, is not impatient either; every storm starts small, and the sudden terrifying earthquake or eruption began in some secret process long before we were made aware of it.

Sometimes a writer achieves a remarkable book in what seems a short time; a composer, a great piece of music; an artist, a wonderful painting. But all these are the flowering of seeds planted years before, the rewards of study and hard work, the sum of experience, the conquering of what has often seemed failure and the daily beginning again.

"God moves in a mysterious way . . ." Did you know Cowper said that? I didn't until I looked it up. And "the mills of God grind slowly . . ." That was Longfellow. . . . Perhaps both men drew on older sources, but the two quotations, which almost everyone knows, stand witness to the basic fact that God doesn't hurry; He isn't impatient.

This is the month when, over a large portion of the country, we expect the hushed or wind-driven white storms; the perilous roads; the beautiful, treacherous ice. Until spring is firmly established, we may reasonably expect that engagements will have to be canceled, cars will stall and accidents befall drivers, passengers and pedestrians. We can expect to be late for an appointment we hold important; that trains won't run on time and planes won't take off. We can expect the milk to be frozen in the bottle if we've forgotten to take it in.

All very frustrating.

Along with impatience, frustration raises the blood pressure. Sometimes we can circumvent, so to speak, the frustrations—if, for instance, the plane is grounded, we can take the train, even if it's going to be late—and that's fine. But when we can't make and carry out substitute plans, let's wait. The storm will cease, the clouds lighten, the roads become, once more, passable.

It's hard to wait for practically anything, even if you're not, by nature, impatient. Yet waiting, if it's hopeful, is an exercise in self-discipline, and a spiritual lesson in trust.

This is the time when half our friends say, "Am I glad another year's begun!" and the other half says, "Thank heaven, the old year's gone!" Perhaps one reaction is positive and the other negative. I don't know. Either way, I suppose, is just an expression of the eternal hope that tomorrow will be better.

There's a lot of glitter around when we announce, on the stroke of midnight, that a new year has made an entrance. But most of us aren't fooled by glitter, lights briefly out, bells, shrieks and celebrations. They're fun in moderation, a sort of "let's give a party for renewal." But we still know that the new year will be very soon, the old, and the baby in the bikini will start growing that beard before many weeks have passed— indeed, almost instantly.

Whether or not you make vows or resolutions, I hope the new year will bless and reward you. I wish to you, and me, a year brilliant with hope, and gentle with patience; one through which we can work, and wait, without self-induced pressures, trusting in ourselves, in life, and in the quiet will and compassionate hands of God.

Bridge

Very soon I am going to run out of metaphorical architectural devices by which I get us from one room, one month, to another. In fact I'm out of them now, so I shall just assume that you, being patient with me, know these short conversations with you are bridges between chapters. When I run out of building material for titles, I'll use whatever comes to hand and mind.

Why can't I just call this one "bridge"? I've always loved bridges.

The big ones, the great spans of steel flung in an arc

across a body of water, frighten me a little. There are some I know quite well: not far from me, the White-stone; and some distance away, the two bridges across the Cape Cod Canal. People native to the Cape, speaking of a trip to another state or even through their own, will say, "I haven't been across the bridge for seven years!" Then there are the bridges which decorate New York City . . . those leading to Brooklyn, to other parts of Long Island; that which goes proudly to New Jersey. The Golden Gate bridge from San Francisco to Oakland is a marvel, as is the bridge across the harbor at Sydney, Australia.

My love, however, is given to little bridges—home-made ones such as we had at the other house which spanned a small brook; bridges in gardens, public and private. In the Hawaiian Islands there are many homes surrounded by Japanese gardens, and there you'll find the miniature bridges. On the island of Molokai I was shown a hula bridge, a swaying structure without hand-rails. I don't remember negotiating it; I'm reasonably sure I did not. Years ago, when I lived in Brooklyn with my family, we used to take the children to the Botanical Garden to see the spring flowers, the cherry blossoms, the iris. It is my recollection that there was such a bridge there, but I may be wrong.

When I was very young, I walked once or twice across Brooklyn bridge, on the pedestrian footpath. I was never a lover of exercise, so I doubt that I did it more often. My brother-in-law, however, used to perform this feat practically every day when he, my sister and their family lived in Brooklyn Heights.

I don't believe there are many big bridges which give the pedestrian room for a stroll or a brisk walk. In any case, it doesn't appeal to me; the water is too far below. But on little bridges in gardens, or built perhaps of a few planks over a stream, I like to loiter. I have stood idly upon many of them and looked into clear water or cloudy, seen flowers growing on the banks, trees crowding down to dip their feet into the stream. It is very easy to linger on a little bridge.

It's rather like living. Almost every day of our lives we cross a little bridge (and sometimes, as the saying runs, burn it behind us), a bridge usually of adjustment from one situation to another. It isn't hard to stay there a moment, an hour, or many hours; not far from either shore while we are making up our minds. Sometimes we can't go back, but we can think about returning.

Upon the big bridges in life—those we cannot possibly burn, those we must cross if we are to go forward, those which seem to be designed for one-way traffic— we cannot stand and dream. It is necessary to cross them in order to get anywhere and, as on the physical bridges, it's a long way down.

Sometimes people jump, rather than cross.

That can happen when you feel you can't go forward; you know you can't go back; and there is no place, no room, no way for you to remain where you are. The long way down seems the short way out.

But it isn't.

It takes a while to learn to cross the big bridges and sometimes even the small, although these present no real threat as a rule, and do not take us into alien country. But learn, we must . . . for what we call death is also a bridge, and from one country to another. . . .

The words on these few pages are just a thinking-on-paper, a small bridge from January to February.

So, we'll cross it.

February

Come in, but do wipe your feet on the beat-up mat
which says *Fable Farm* because, if you carry the least
sliver of ice on your shoes—or more practical galoshes
—you'll fall flat on your face when you attempt these
old floors. They aren't too highly waxed or polished,
but here and there they wave a little, warped with the
years. Last spring, a woman who'd been writing me for
some time (we have the same birthday date and year)
but whom I'd never met, person to person, came to see
me. She wore the highest heels I ever saw, made of

metal, thinned down almost to a needle point. She didn't fall, but several times caught her heel between the wide old boards, and once we had to take her out of her shoe, her husband and I. What this did to the boards we won't discuss, and it probably scared her—but not, I daresay, into lowering the standards of her heels.

Me—anything more than a wedgie on my feet, and I fall down, standing up.

This is a chancy month. It can do just about anything; produce the earliest little flowers under the melting snow, or pile the snow right up to the window sills. It can bring ice storms, which I dread for all their beautiful glitter and fairy-tale charm under a sunny sky—or under a gray one the effect of static smoke. At the other house, we lost more trees in an ice storm than in two hurricanes.

Also, now, is the time of sleet, winds, draughts and the respiratory ailments flesh seems heir to—yet again, as in every month, there is loveliness.

Sometimes February seems to symbolize itself. The leafless boughs have clustered snow clinging to them, which sometimes looks like popcorn balls and sometimes like the white bloom of a cherry tree. But nowhere do I see Mr. Washington's legendary axe. Lincoln, whose portrait, an old steel engraving, hangs in my study—just to my left as I write—has a spiritual counterpart in the great trunks of trees, standing firm against storm. And every day, in the red of the cardinal against the snow, I am confronted with a valentine redder than any heart.

This is a nice birthday month. People preen themselves a little if their birthdays fall on the twelfth or twenty-second. And those who celebrate the fourteenth have every excuse to be sentimental. I have a friend who celebrates hers on the twenty-ninth, or once in four years, and if she counts only the actual dates, isn't she fortunate? It seems anyway to have kept her young in spirit.

Our February roads are usually chunked or coated with ice so that, looking from a window, I hesitate to go out on foot or by car (I don't drive, but my friends do; also taximen). I'm chicken, I suppose. On foot I am as unsteady as the hula bridge I spoke of, and in a car I hold my breath until I am apt to turn blue. But I have never been a back-seat or any other kind of driver.

Well, I suppose living at all is somewhat like that; dangerous, after the positive decision; or negative in hesitation, with duty perhaps sacrificed for safety.

What will tomorrow be like? I have never trusted weather reports (my apologies to the Bureau). Will we have sleet, freezing rain, snow flurries, a blizzard or that wonderful pale blue sky with a seashell yellow sun which sometimes accompanies February . . . a calm sky, so we can forget the bitter winds of late?

Some of my readers have written to ask me certain questions. "Are you ever discouraged?" they inquired. "Are you always as serene as you appear to be in print?"

It is necessary to be honest. I heard a great person say recently, "Always stand firm upon the truth." So, here goes.

The answer to the first question is yes; and to the second, no.

We live, whether we know it or not, simultaneously upon two levels of consciousness—the outward and the inward, the physical and the spiritual. Only a few people in the history of the world, I imagine, have achieved a whole self, integrated, with absolute freedom from discouragement, and with a serenity which is complete, both inside and out. Only a few have been able to divorce themselves from anxiety, sorrow and responsibility—as well as joy—and to remove from their consciousness all the frustrations, limitations, disappointments and worries implicit in life upon earth. Every person *I* have ever known, however rooted in marvelous trust in God—with which some are born and others win with difficulty and frequent backsliding—is often cast down, has dark moods and desperate hours. I am many times discouraged, mainly about myself and my failures in endeavors or relationships, or about people I love who are going through something hard to endure. Therefore, on the surface, which is where we at least appear to live during our waking hours, I am often as unquiet as the February day.

Few escape; and in the black hours it seems useless to tell ourselves—however true—that this, too, will pass; that this also is a lesson to be learned.

It will; and it is; but there are moments when words are just words without more than the dictionary meaning.

One thing is certain: if we can alter the circumstance which threatens to defeat us, that is our responsibility; if we cannot, and know it is God's will, we can, however unhappily, accept it.

Sometimes I feel that I'm mistreated; that I have waited too long for the telephone which didn't ring, the letter which didn't come; that I have suffered too many vigils during nights and days when someone I loved lay critically ill or upon an operating table.

Yet, in recent years, I know—as truly as I know I am breathing at this very moment—I have achieved an inner quietude which is undisturbed by the procession of outer events. I have learned painfully, if not wholly, to retreat within this fortress when matters go wrong beyond any remedial measure of my own, past any effort I can make, and beyond my comprehension as well. This is the lull in the February storm, the gentling of the wind, the essential safety, warmth and the breaking through the light.

When I, in print, appear undisturbed, it is because I know I should be, and that, in my essence, I am, for I am writing of truth and spiritual law. I do not always in my behavior express or obey these, for I am like almost everyone else, fallible, weak and many times mistaken. So there is no formula I can give anyone, beyond the expression of what I believe to be truth. And nothing I can teach. But there's a lot I can learn. So, I try.

Now, in New England we bundle up, eyes, ears, feet, but the heart can be worn on the sleeve if you want to risk it. It's the season of hearts and flowers (even if they bloom under the sheltered south window), so hearts are trumps. *Tête-à-tête* is a pleasant, common phrase for confidential conversation but "heart to heart" is a better one. No matter what one is saying aloud, we know at times that human spirits speak silently to one another.

What a wonderful word *heart* is and capable of how many interpretations! We sign ourselves to someone we love, "with all my heart"; we speak, when sorrowful, of "a heavy heart"; we remark, when we're doing something without pleasure, "My heart's not in it."

Everyone, in discussing an issue says, sooner or later, the "heart of the matter" is this or that; and we urge our friends when faced with trouble to "take heart." My sister talks of the heart—or the mother leaves—of her superb African violets. When something happens to us, a blow, a treachery, a disloyalty, we are "struck to the heart." But when doctors talk of cardiac diseases, developments and difficulties, they, too, are speaking of the heart. It's a somber word, then.

The physical heart is a muscle, working twenty-four hours a day under stress and often neglected or over-driven by its owner. But when we say to someone, "You are my heart," we aren't thinking of the small pump which beats, sometimes falters and, at the end of one's task, ceases to function.

The books you remember and reread have heart in them and when the poet speaks to his love he says, in every language, "my heart, my soul."

In prayer, we ask that mind and heart be cleansed and we are told that the broken and the contrite heart the Lord will not despise.

Since time immemorial men have spoken and written of broken hearts. I, for one, believe they do break, or at least often crack a little, no matter in what excellent health the body's heart may be. We speak also of gay hearts, and kind, of those which are loving and giving, and when we walk in spring and summer gardens we sometimes recall that the flowers we know as pansies were originally called heart's-ease.

Sometimes someone says of another that his manner may be awkward or brusque or cold, but his heart is good; or conversely that So-and-so seems to be a very pleasant person, but there is evil in his heart.

When we sit with friends and speak of a trouble uppermost in our minds, we are easing our hearts, and when we are grateful beyond any word for the answered prayer or the strong arm in time of distress, we say, our hearts overflow. . . . So it's not all written on the valentines, which according to custom we open on the fourteenth.

The physical history of the human heart is written in medical books and papers: what it is, what enemies can attack it, what remedies can be used, what the diagnosis is for this or that condition, and the prognosis. More and more we read of miraculous heart surgery and unremitting research; but the history of what the word "heart" symbolizes is in every book ever written, whether great or good, mediocre or even downright bad, as far as literary values are concerned. Nor has the last word been said; not in medicine or in any other way. For the human spirit is still a mystery; though the heart has been explored, it too, has its mysteries, known only to its Creator.

When we obey unconsciously, the admonition to let our light so shine, it is the light of the heart as well as of the soul. I know this when a friend comes into the room saying nothing unusual yet bearing with him, or her, that warmth and reassurance which is from the heart and which is indeed a light.

In Great Britain a cup of tea seems to be the remedy for almost all shocks and surprises. I, too, find it so; and we speak of it—as of many other things—as heartening. So now, perhaps we should have tea. We can close the inside shutters against the sudden unpredicted fall of snow, and, as a special gesture put a match to the kindling and logs and the pine cones. We don't need the added heat, but a fire on the hearth singing above the wind and talking brightly to itself—for a hearth fire has its own brief, secret life—is friendly, and warms more than hands or feet. I like to see its glancing flicker, as I draw the pink curtains and sit down to make my confession that many times—like all people unless they are superhuman—I whistle in the dark.

Now, we can warm our hands around the blue and white rice-grain porcelain cups, which came from China, and listen for the chickadees, if they have ventured out, for the windows are open at the top. If this day were bright, hands could be warmed in the sun at the south windows and the cardinal might be scarlet, flashing to the feeder.

The heart, I suppose, has its own thermostat, and if we trust, it can be set to rise when the mental or emotional temperature goes down.

Whatever I say to you in these pages is honest, or as honest as I can make it. Who knows himself, or his motives? I do not always practice what I preach. Who does? But even failing, I know that what I preach is valid. I do not know all the answers. I know actually very few. But being just like everyone else is extremely consoling. For now and then I come to an understanding of people; and I am sure many understand me. It has not been my lot, or even my desire, to withdraw from ordinary living; to stand above the crowd, to keep myself uninvolved. Ivory towers must be exquisite, but can you build a hearth fire in an ivory tower? Most towers are high and, except in airplanes, I don't like heights, or looking down.

For better or worse, I am what I have made of myself, with the materials God gave me. Each of us is just that; each of us is really self-made and when we look back and see what an incompetent job we've done, we can be somewhat if not entirely comforted by the fact that almost everyone else, sooner or later, thinks the same thing of himself.

Now in the Deep South spring is thinking of making an entrance, and Down Under, it's still summer. But in any climate or section or language the heart speaks out,

in word and action, in art, in work, in human relationships . . . sometimes for evil but more often for good.

I write frequently to several children overseas—Ko-
rean, Japanese, Greek, German and French—and to an
American Indian boy, and to children in several rural
Kentucky schools. None has ever seen me. Only the
American Indian and the Kentucky youngsters speak
my own country's language. But heart speaks to heart.

In the hall is the Sung bowl which often has a plant
in it, or now, since autumn, the gourds. I'll take them
out and put the valentines in, and over there on the desk
is a valentine nosegay, with a paper frill, in the ame-
thyst glass vase.

So there's the fireplace and here's the tea; we can
smell the roses, look at the cards. And may you in
your mail have many a paper heart and in the heart
which lives within you courage, laughter and trust.

Be then, my Valentine.

An archway

I have designed an archway between February and March, so that there's a little space as we cross from the very wintery winter month into one apt to ape her predecessor in weather but, nevertheless, forced to lead us to spring.

I doubt if many archways contain bookshelves, but I don't see why these can't. We can scoop it out a little; and think about the books we have loved, the books we always meant to read and haven't, the books we hope people will write for us.

My turn first.

Alice is there, in her wonderland and also through the looking glass; she makes a rather odd shelf companion for Undset's trilogy, *Kristin Lavransdatter*. But that's the way they are placed in my bedroom bookcase and I can't seem to break the habit. I suspect that more adults than children read *Alice*. If they don't, they should. Sometimes when I hurry too much, I think of myself as the White Rabbit, although I rarely have a *pair* of clean white gloves . . . just one, if any at all.

Which reminds me of some twenty-one years ago when a friend and I made the long trip Down Under. We had to attend a lot of receptions and gloves were necessary. But we found we had only one pair between us; elegantly, we each carried a glove.

The Bible is in the archway bookcase; I have a number of copies, but this one is small and worn and my younger son gave it to me long ago. And also there is *The Prophet* by Kahlil Gibran. . . . Since I first encountered this book many years ago, one quotation from it has been written in every address book I've ever owned, for, as you know, I frequently consult my address book. Last year, my younger daughter decorated and illuminated the quotation for me—illuminating words and over them a painting of trees and mountains and a road. It hangs in my study to the right of the mantelpiece.

Also on the shelf, Bhagavad-gītā. I treasure it not
only because of the profound meaning which lies within
it, but also because it was part of my youth. My name
is in it and the date 1910. I had, at that time, an extraordinary English and history teacher; this book was one
of our assignments; and along the margins and at the
bottom of pages I find my own notes, written in a
curly, affected hand. They must have been taken down
from Miss Adams's explanations, for when I started to
reread it a year or so ago, I had rather hard going until
I began consulting my notes.

Somewhere along the shelves are two novels: one
called *The Corn King and the Spring Queen*, by Naomi
Mitchison, a story of vanished antiquity and magic; and
the other Winifred Holtby's *South Riding*. And scat-
tered among the other books there'll be several by my
beloved friend Storm Jameson. And most certainly, a
couple of mysteries, a Josephine Tey, for instance, and
my favorite Dorothy Sayers . . . *Busman's Honey-
moon*.

The archway won't contain all the books which I
reread. I won't say I reread all those now in this house.
But, a good many. When I moved from the other house,
I had to give away some two thousand or more. There's
not much room here—though recently I found spaces
in two guest rooms, the upper hall and a back room, as
my children have finally gotten around to taking to

their own homes the books they cherished. Deciding what books I must keep when I moved, was difficult. I had for a long time collected, in their original editions, many English writers and had shelves of their books, not all published here. So I kept a few of each. I had a wonderful collection of John Buchan and I gave all but a couple of them, I think, to one of my sons. Recently I missed them and the first thing you know my favorite out-of-print book shop was scouring the country for me until I had an even more complete collection than before (in all kinds of bindings and editions).

So I took time off, evenings, to reread them; and for the first time read some I hadn't had before.

About every ten years I try to straighten out the shelves; the fiction, nonfiction, the books autographed to me, the editions I bought already signed, the books I've used in research, the second-hand books I bought long ago wondering if any were worth a fortune. (None was.)

I somehow doubt I'll tackle the job again except, perhaps, in very small stages.

In life we go from one month to another of the year; in books we are not hampered by time, space or calendars. We can go forward in time or we can go back; those of us who were reading children can return to the wonder of our childhood and our adolescence. I've kept some of the most unlikely books at which critics would now shudder, simply because of the joy they gave me when first I read them.

We can go not only backward and forward but up and down. Some of the great books are dark, most of them tragic, but some are hopeful about man's ultimate destination.

Before I take a look at March I'll put some poetry on the archway shelves. There should be poetry in every month. I like mine lyric; some light, and some not; I am afraid, as in music, I prefer the minor key. I have never been enthralled by great epic poetry, or by many narrative poems.

In your own daily living take books with you from one month into the next; old friends and new. Mine stay with me from one year's end to another's and will for as long as I'll be reading. I'm happy when I buy a new book, read it, and find I'd like to keep it and not give it away. There haven't been too many of these, in the past few years, for me. As I said, I haven't room here to keep anything except what I really want.

I think I'll take a field guide to the birds with me into March. The birds will be coming back; and I'll also filch from the archway bookcase my volume of Rupert Brooke. He loved the spring.

March

In New England, in March you don't drop in, you blow in. Regarding this uncertain month with a wary, if expectant eye, I manage to remind myself that in our South, spring is blooming—Deep South, fully; Medium South, less—and that in my lovely Down Under it's autumn. In England, too, it's spring, on the southern coast; and in many parts of the world where I've never been.

Here, it can be anything: hot or cold, mild or freezing, raining or snowing. You pay your money and have no choice. It doesn't matter very much. Once it's March, you're close to April.

I recall a long-ago March evening, the day before my older son was born, when I walked with extreme reluctance and exaggerated care, between city-dirty banks of snow. High, too. And was scared as a rabbit of falling.

Whatever the season, it flows inexorably into the next. Airplane travel produces within a few hours the illusion of being catapulted into another month or season. No, not an illusion. It's real. You leave San Juan or Jamaica on a breathless, tropic-hot morning in March and presently you land in snow and sleet and are greeted by an icy wind. It's incredible. I've done it.

Sometimes I wish myself back in the slower era of the horse and buggy, the cranked telephone, the gas lights. Born as I was before the twentieth century, I remember all this. I also recall the first automobile and the first airplane I ever saw, as well as, later, the crystal radio set to which I listened with passionate interest and unbelief. I haven't, personally, caught up with the times. I've still no idea how the telephone works, and the mechanics of motors are unsolved mysteries. So how am I to understand radio, let alone airplanes and television?

Actually, I don't want to . . . I feel much as I do in

the presence of a good magician, amateur or professional. Unlike the majority of the audience who yearn to know how it's done, I don't want to know. I simply accept and enjoy.

Acceptance is half the battle of living in peace with yourself and your neighbors. I don't mean, for instance, that I've liked accepting noises to which I've been unaccustomed, such as the sudden wild barking of dogs under hitherto quiet windows. But accept I must. I've never personally met these roaming dog people, or the cats for that matter; but every living four-footed creature within miles seems attracted to my few acres, so I lean out of windows and beg them to go away, and leave the pheasants and other birds alone.

When first I moved to this house, there was nothing in back of the property to disturb anyone and nothing opposite me save one dwelling and an old barn. The barn went in due time and the snarl and whine of bulldozers came, and now there are several houses across the road, from which children emerge to catch the school bus. Unfortunately, two of my bedroom windows look out upon the road. I was brought up to open windows at night and I have no deaf ear to turn to the pillow; my hearing is sufficiently acute.

Cars drive into the private roads opposite and one neighbor for a reason I've never been able to fathom (and as I don't know him, I can't ask) keeps garage and lamppost lights burning all night. The reflections dance on my hitherto mercifully dark walls. But, if I close my eyes—and you're supposed to, if you're to sleep—I can't see them. On the rare occasions when I sleep past eight o'clock I'm tired enough to dream through school buses, uproar, shouts and the birdlike voices of the young.

This is progress, this tumult, and who am I to complain of it? I have sufficient property upon which to erect the ivory tower we spoke of, back a few pages. But where do I get the ivory and besides you know I wouldn't like it.

The lesson of acceptance is one of the hardest to learn. I've been working on it for quite a spell, and cannot yet rate myself as A or even B. To accept change, slow or sudden, to accept the inevitable alterations in one's life, even in one's way of living or thinking, isn't easy; and to accept other people's inviolable right to opinions other than your own is hard, too.

To accept God's will, even if you do not understand it—and few of us do—is the most difficult, yet rewarding of all acceptances. Those of us who say the Lord's Prayer—formally at religious gatherings, aloud in a quiet room, or mentally to ourselves—rarely stop to think about each word and sentence or ponder on its strong core of inner meaning. To me the four words, *Thy Will be done*, are the most important; and they are valid in every creed.

Blind faith is something we've heard about as long as we remember. I do not think this is the ultimate in belief. Unless his small personal world has been shattered, the faith of a child in his parents and in his total security is blind until he begins to think for himself, at which point reason gives blind faith its sight. An adult's faith must be logical and based upon an immutable foundation, which gives him the capacity, when for him the world is shattered, to go a step beyond the bewildered child and accept loss or alteration.

This being March, most of my friends announce that they are feeling depressed; the winter's been long, hard and busy, and spring isn't here as yet. Some of them experience this slump as early as January and, if they can afford it, take off for the semitropics or a cruise. Many people get the go-away virus in February, and go if they can, or wait if they must. Those who plan a March vacation embark, entrain, motor or fly away in triumph and return in about two weeks to two feet of snow. They tell us they hate March.

You know, or think you know, more or less, what to expect of other months, but March has a whole bagful of tricks: bluster, wind, rain, snow—and also the sudden warm melting days, very like a girl's heart, which she believed adamant—and a strange look about the trees, which is promising, even if there isn't so far a hint of green.

If March is a mishmash of abrupt storm, driving sleet and overnight ice, I still know that April must follow, and after that comes May. So if I complain—and I always do—I can accept, wait and think: This, too, will pass.

In California the hills are greening and on the deserts the lovely carpet of spring flowers will spread. In the Far South people are turning on fans and the scent of blossoms is everywhere. I am happy to remember that, over the years, I have seen these miracles of returning life in many places.

I don't really think of March as a deliberately deceiving period. It's an in-between-season month; so it behaves like yesterday's winter and tomorrow's spring.

March is in a way, a sergeant; it's giving-orders month; also a good, busy, housekeeper month. You know. Clean house. Rake up the winter-fallen branches. Take a look at what will be flower beds. Mend the fences. Paint the window boxes. Put on your raincoat. Take off your jacket. Keep your galoshes handy. Don't send the heavy coats to storage, yet. Get out a thin dress and hang it beside the woolens. You honestly don't know from one day to the next what the weather will be like.

Remember the Scout motto: Be prepared.

Shamrocks and sunshine; wind and weather; rain, which is a penetration of the iron frost; snow and mud; and always the wind-blown puddles, bright blue on a blue bright day. The forsythia branches toss in the wind and March says, "Why don't you cut some and bring them in the house?"

Do this and in no time at all you'll have a shower of gold.

I have to do a good deal of birthday-book checking this month. One year, seized with a horrible fit of forward-looking efficiency, I bought birthday cards, addressed and filed them in just the right pocket file for each month, with dates and names carefully written below. A friend had given me this helpful, attractive gadget—a file which remembered for you. It didn't, for me. In order for it to remember, *I* had to. I set it on a shelf and forgot it. So when important dates approached, I dredged them up from my memory, sent other cards and afterwards found those I had already addressed.

Oh, well, there's always another year.

If I were offered a role—and could write it—in a horror movie (and why not?), I should create it with care, and it would be that of The Mad Organizer. Unfortunately, organizing sometimes backfires, and when that happens, complete disorganization sets in.

Perhaps this month I'll discover a door which pleasantly opens upon moderation.

I've always been inclined to the immoderate in worry, in looking back and reliving. I'm trying to overcome this, as it avails me nothing.

It appears to be the average man's lot to spend most of his waking hours in anxiety: about himself, someone else, his own trouble or that of another, about circumstances or events. Much that we anguish about in advance never happens, and even if it does, worry is not constructive. Yet worry we must if we are overly burdened or oppressed, or if someone we love is in trouble. I haven't found a formula against this except in words. I know the constructive thing is to do something about whatever claws at us. I know that sitting still and wringing the mental hands accomplishes nothing. I still worry, though not as much as formerly.

I remember very long ago when two people I loved were very ill and in different hospitals. Neither knew of the other's danger and one was too young to understand, had he known. I spent my days going with a stabilizing rock-strong friend between hospitals. Evenings, I worked, as work was imperative and constructive and would, if I were fortunate, enable me to help.

It is harder to meet such a challenge when you are twice as old; the body is less adaptable, the mind less flexible, and even less hopeful; you tire more easily and the reasoning power falters at decisions. But to these conditions also we must adjust, accepting them.

This delightful house has four outside doors, one of which leads downward into the cellar. The three other doors are confusing. If you ring the chimes at the side door which, at the end of a brick path, leads into a little hall, or the kitchen door, opening off the back porch reached by another brick path, I'll come to the wrong one. The chimes are different, I'm told, but I don't seem to have learned. We don't use the third door, which for other generations, long ago, was the front door. There's a set of stone steps, and a stone landing with ironwork around it. Random-placed flat stones once led down over the grass to a stone wall, where there were more steps to the public road. I closed up the wall. I like the side door.

When people come to the original front door—and many do, although I don't know why, as the driveway is nowhere near it—they can't ring a bell. There isn't any. They just purely hammer and peer through the two very long narrow panes of glass. So I look through my study window and make signs, if winter, or shout, if summer, requesting that they go around to the kitchen or side door. For if I let them in at the front, they'd be in a hall the size of a tea tray, with the dining room left, the study right, and smack dab in front of them the enclosed stairway.

Perhaps I should have only one house door, for at times—on Halloween, for instance—I nearly lose my mind.

But mentally, it seems to me, we all should have a number of doors. We can't go through life letting people in by one way only.

There are doors of understanding, of compassion, of sympathy and, better still, empathy. There are doors through which people may freely enter and find warmth, laughter, quietude or strength and these should be open to friend and stranger. Through them we can also leave our own small, personal, restricted world to go in search of something we do not possess— wisdom perhaps, or courage, a larger viewpoint, a greater comprehension.

A man came to this house of wood the other day. He had business in the cellar. Actually he was looking for termites, which must be an unhappy sort of occupation. One or another from the company he works for has come annually ever since someone did find termites. There haven't been any since, I'm happy to report.

A door chime rang. I was alone and busy. I went muttering to the kitchen door and, peering out across the terrace, saw him at the other door, the side one. He came over by stepping catty-corner across the terrace. I took him to the inside cellar steps which crouch behind a door, hidden by a Chinese screen, at one end of the oddly shaped living room.

I was cross.

I folded back the screen which was my grandmother's (it is perfectly beautiful: teakwood and, under glass, embroidery—and weighs a ton), opened the cellar door and touched the switch of the cellar lights. Nothing happened. The man produced a flashlight and we went down. Patiently he traced the two lights which were on the switch and removed the bulbs. I plodded upstairs, found new bulbs, and he put them where they belonged. This was far beyond the call of termite duty.

Later, I let him out the side door, past the table and the Copenhagen, the old pattern-glass lamp and grandfather's portrait. But we'd a good chat first.

I'd let him in at a wrong door, metaphorically speaking—the door of impatience and "Oh, why must I be interrupted?" and, "Why can't he be at the door I've trudged to?"

If he hadn't come—by any door—I wouldn't have found out about the cellar lights for a day or two and maybe someone would have fallen downstairs.

So he left and I returned to my work. The job I was

doing wasn't terribly important, but I came back to it refreshed from the termite break, and with the feeling that a stranger had done me a very real service.

We learn our lessons at the oddest times and in the most unlikely circumstances.

So come in, side door, or kitchen—it doesn't matter.

When evening falls, if the night is clear, the wind will blow the clouds from the stars and polish them to a special brilliance. Under the cold, still-frozen earth young roots and old are stirring, and the bulbs are thinking of beauty. Birds are returning every day to the feeders; ducks sail across the sky in battle formation. Every revolution of the earth upon its axis brings new marvel.

Man, in seeking to conquer outer space, has forgotten that he has not yet conquered himself, or solved all his problems with his neighbors across the street, the nation or the seas. Advancement in the understanding of spiritual laws lags far behind that of science. Maybe it will always be so. I do not know.

I do know that on a March day, at morning or noontide or dusk, the door may blow open for you or shut behind you, but it's warm inside and there is welcome, whether March is behaving like a lion or a lamb.

Let us talk about what a winter we've had and what a spring is on the way—the greening bough, the homing bird. Let's open a window and listen to the birds telling each other of their journeys, and vacations, and to the sergeant's annual command.

Forward, March!

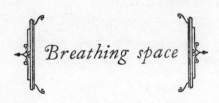

Breathing space

Let's take a good deep breath and pretend, as you put your little foot forward, that you are poised between month and month. What happened just now? What is going to happen in a minute or so?

What happens to me between the twinkle of one month and the next is a firm belief that things will be better—and also that we are nearer to something. Long ago I dreaded the autumn, sliding in flame toward winter; but it's easy now to think of that in another way; much nearer, I tell myself, to my birthday, to Thanksgiving, to Christmas. And when March comes—well it's close to Easter, whether Easter comes in March or April.

This sounds, I think, extremely Pollyanna, but isn't really, for as you grow older, time hurries and you don't think, as you did when young, that the distance between month and month, holiday and holiday, Christmas and summer is practically forever.

Children have a different notion of time. I remember the daughter who told me gravely, when I was in my forties, that I was "very well preserved"; and her twin brother who, highly interested in the pioneer covered wagon, or as he put it "olden days," asked, "You remember them, don't you, Mom?"

Time's a deceiver. But I was crushed.

Opposite my typewriter, which sits at right angles to the desk—I have to swing around to write, illegibly by hand—there is a crane on the mantelpiece. This is new, a Christmas gift; slender and delicately poised, the tall bird is hand-carved of an East Indian wood, very dark, exceedingly smooth to the touch. I put it there with the Kwan Yin, the Buddha and other things I cherish. But only after a few days of glancing up at it from my typewriter did I appreciate the polish and craftsmanship, and especially the stretched, graceful line of the long neck—the upward looking.

The crane is a familiar symbol in Chinese myth and folklore. I don't know what it represents in India.

Last January, during the thaw, when the air was so like spring that you ran out to see if you could cut the forsythia for house-forcing, my sister drove up unexpectedly and we had lunch in a place I have known for twenty-four years. It's an old tavern, on a river which is always full of ducks. On this day, they were sitting on the banks, on the ice where it was thickest, and swimming where there was no ice; there were hundreds of them, mostly mallards.

I remembered then—for somehow there is a continuity to everything—that just before my younger son went off to the Navy in the Second (and I pray last) World War, we took him there for lunch. It must have been in the spring. We sat at a table overlooking the river and watched the ducks. There was a Mama Duck, a multitude of babies, and Papa, who brought up the rear. They swam in formation, but one little guy, apparently a rebel, kept breaking away and going off in very unsteady circles and V's on his own.

It was fun to watch Mama come along and herd him back until he swam with the pack and toward the shore.

There were thirteen of the babies. Every time I went to the tavern, thereafter, I would watch for them and report by mail, to Stephen, at camp before taking off for the Pacific, how many were left.

Ducks are expendable. Perhaps there are in the river, as in other small bodies of water in my district, big turtles which destroy them.

So, sitting with my sister watching the many birds, motionless or swimming,—they won't all stay of course —I was back in time a good many years.

The days flow into weeks and weeks into months. The poet who requested Time to turn backward needn't have asked; it does, every day.

It's not a continuous flowing forward, it's a circle and you can retrace events—yet not remedy mistakes —and keep on.

My sister must have wondered why I was silent for a space of time; I am usually extremely garrulous. But I had suddenly become a good many years younger and a boy who is now a man, a husband and father, seemed to be standing beside me, counting ducks, and I was wondering—and trying not to—if ever he would stand there again.

He did.

So pause, for a breather, look back and look ahead. The past and the present and the future are inextricably around us, always.

April

Don't just stand there; come in. Of course I ran to the wrong door. Someday I'm going to have chimes that will direct me. "Back door," one will sing; and, "Front," the other. Oh, well, racing from one to another keeps one thin, or at least, active.

I never know what an April visitor will bring in: sun, rain, fog—we have lots of fog here—sleet, chill, or almost-summer warmth.

April is a kitten: quick and caressing, or hostile; she'll either purr or scratch.

She advances as a kitten does, she retreats, and sulks in a corner, and cannot be coaxed out to play. Then, when suddenly the sunlight comes pouring in, she catches it in her paws. Now and again she rolls a white yarn ball across the room; we call it "unexpected snow."

I like kittens and I like April; unpredictable, a trifle zany—one moment purring in your ear, all sleek, warm charm, and the next spitting at you across the room or unleashing claws from velvet pads.

This year Easter's just past midmonth; maybe we can wear new suits—or last year's best as I intend to do—and go without a topcoat. There's always a chance, however, of having to wrap ourselves in woolens. It matters very little. Those of us who live in a mild climate can parade in April without worry; the New Englander, the Northerner—that's another story. But for us all, it's going to be Easter.

Last autumn we had the bulb garden under the south window dug up as it was old and tired. We put in new soil and new bulbs. Almost immediately our extremely busy moles ate them up. I think they sit under the shade of juniper trees, or peer up from underground through periscopes—don't tell me they're blind—and watch what's going on. I bet those moles all got together, crying, "Goody, goody!"

So we put in more bulbs; and during a warm spell last

winter they proceeded to appear above ground; after which, naturally, they froze back. In late January, during the thaw, some of them popped up again. Now I can't wait to see what will come up—if anything.

Oh well, easy come, easy go.

The robins have returned. They always send a lone, advance courier and a few days later I look out and there are fifty or a hundred of them flocking. Now those who have decided to spend spring and summer at this motel have settled in and stand cocking invisible ears, listening to sounds as of stirring of life, the whisper of promise at the root, the admonition to branch and leaf: *It's time, it's time.*

In April, walking under the trees, I can see the green silently creeping along boughs so recently dark and bare; it's almost invisible, this tranquil return of life, but inevitably it is there.

This is a giving month . . . I have no idea what those who cross the threshold will bring to me from outdoors: a left-over March wind, a streak of February sleet, a sunburst of warmth borrowed from a future June, or a handful of snowdrops and crocuses. It's a birthday month for many who are dear to me. I've scarcely recovered from the procession of March birthdays—the son, the grandchild, the Shamrock friend—when April reminds me to get busy, shopping, wiring, card sending. Gladys Taber is an April child; so is my agent who deciphers my madhouse typing as, one by one, I send her manuscripts. In this month, too, my only sister was born, as was a friend up north who collects pattern glass; and my twins are April children.

Terribly tough on the budget; but fun.

April is a sighing deep within the branch and a flickering of wings. Snow, showers or sunlight, the promise is always there. People who live in northern climates get so tired of winter. For however beautiful, it is stark, often violent, and seeming endless. Even in more temperate climates there is also a winter season—although some tourists don't believe it—and in the semitropics. It doesn't express itself as it does here, yet it speaks in storm or chill, or rain. Here, when winter's over, there's an out-of-the-moth-balls feeling, a buzz of waking wasps in the attic—they usually find their way downstairs—a singing sweep of the sort of rain which grows things, fast, especially if the sun comes tumbling after; and there's always, from March on, the housekeeping wind pulling down dead branches and busily sweeping everything before it.

It's like that often with the human spirit. My grandmother used to speak of being "dispirited." Nowadays, we say, "depressed" and in-between generations said, "out of sorts." But the soul knows its own seasons. They may not coincide with Nature's, but they're explicit: the winter darkness; the days of storm, and those of calm and light. Here, too, as in Nature there is always the promise, the flexing of spiritual muscles, and the turning toward growth.

In the Christian faith, Easter is a thoughtful remembering; and in the Feast of the Passover, also. In all countries when it is spring, there is the inward religious significance, and the outward show of flowers.

No matter what our creed, we learn, sometimes painfully, that the holidays we celebrate on days set aside are really with us always, a remembering of other times —the Easter sunrise, the Christmas carol, the Festival of Lights, the New Year and the Passover; and the holy days observed by Moslem, Brahman, and Buddhist— for all holy days are kept not merely on a calendar but in remembering hearts.

I know this to be true for I have, in June, celebrated the giving warmth of Christmas and in November the springtime dawn.

All matters of time and space are incomprehensible to me. My oldest grandchild—she'll be nine soon— knows more about them than I, for I do not have a mathematical mind. I recall crossing, for the first time, by ship, the equator and the international date line. We lost a Sunday. Where did it go? I felt cheated. Sunday's a wonderful day for sleeping late, for lazy speculations over coffee, for churchgoing, meditation, and making excuses not to work. Coming back, also by ship, we picked up an extra Thursday. What's Thursday? It's only—in households fortunate enough to have someone other than the mistress in the kitchen—Cook's day out.

Many years later, I crossed the Pacific by air, and then flew from Australia to London and back again over the Atlantic. In this world swing, I lost a day, in bits and pieces, and then it was returned to me—but not in one sensible solid twenty-four-hour lump, to which I could give a name. No sir. More bits and pieces, an hour here, an hour there—half an hour, two hours. Me, I thought I'd lost that day forever.

I didn't, of course. For nothing's forever lost: not a good impulse or a bad; not a kind thought or an unkind, not a person you've ever loved, not one thought or deed or wish. Whatever sidereal time states—and I don't know anything about sidereal time—or psychological time indicates, eternity encompasses us.

Now that it's spring I think back to other springs, happy, uncertain or miserable. They're still with me, whatever the calendar says.

Most of my life, I've been a writing woman and if you write—however badly, indifferently or inadequately—you must feel, and you must observe. Therefore, you are aware that no season is just exactly like any which has gone before. Nor is any person you meet exactly like someone met yesterday, last week, last year, a dozen years ago. Everyone is unique. And even the person you met yesterday isn't just as he was last week or as he will be tomorrow.

Some time ago I spoke to a group of writers in another part of the country. Maybe they didn't like what I said. In other talks, by writers and editors, there had been an enormous amount of emphasis upon creative writing, its importance, as well as the importance of the other forms of expression. I could not agree with them that work in what we call "the arts" is the most important creative manifestation. None agreed with me either, but I was, at least, honest according to my lights.

Any talent is a God-gift and no person with talent, be it large or small, can take the slightest credit for it. He simply cannot help it. If, as people point out, it's heredity—well, it had to begin somewhere, didn't it? Six fingers on one hand are unusual, but if you have them, you can't help that either. (Did you ever see a double-pawed kitty? I did recently, and was it ever clumsy-cute!)

It is what a person does with his talent that counts; and the only credit a creative worker can take is for hard, unremitting work itself, and the necessary self-discipline which is part of it. I do not go along with far more intellectual people than myself in the premise that a "true artist would murder his wife, rob his mother and starve his children in order to create." Maybe he would, but I'd be much more interested in what pos-

sessed his wife, mother and children to permit such go-
ings on than I would in anything he could produce.

I'm so sick and tired of hearing people say, "Of
course I'm just a housewife . . ."or maybe, "Well I'm
just the man in the street."

Why, *just?*

I am deeply grateful for the marvelous gifts of creative minds and hands in any field—literature, theater,
painting, music. Through them the world which reads
and looks and listens has gained so much down through
the ages. People's vision has been expanded, their imagi-
nations have been stirred, their spirits lifted. Still I cannot agree that even the most magnificent form of art is
the greatest act of creativity.

Our world is that—the earth, the people on it, of all
races, creeds and conditions—and we know the Creator.

Next to this, I think, is family life; the good, solid,
tender, give-and-take relationship between a man and
his wife; the creating and bringing up of good children.
There are millions of such families; they don't make the
headlines, and the analyst's couch rarely receives them.
In a selective sense there are only a handful of really
great artists, living, today. Are we not lucky that the
numbers aren't reversed?

Though genius is rare, talent is far from extraordinary, and it has as many degrees as a thermometer. But
I am convinced that any human relationships, which

have become as nearly perfect as human relationships can be, are more an expression of the Creator than anything Shakespeare wrote, Beethoven composed or Rembrandt painted.

Looking out the window and wondering about bulbs I think, too, of the creative earth.

Years ago, before World War Two, I owned—or was owned by—a lot more acreage than I have here, and I had people to work in house and grounds. The gardener often became agitated. With expert, loving care he would plant peas, beans, asparagus, lettuce— and as soon as they ventured above ground along came the deer (it's forbidden to shoot them in this state, thank goodness!) or pheasants, woodchuck or what- ever and neatly nipped down the rows. Once, having reached the end of his patience, he asked me what he was to do, and I brightly replied, "Plant enough for us all—for us, for you, for the birds and animals."

So he did.

He stayed with us during most of the war and we were able to take masses of vegetables to the community canning kitchen, which supplied not only us and the gardener's family and our friends but contributed to the lunch program of the local school—and there were still things growing for bird and deer.

I am a believer in sufficient supply for everyone; and always the balance; not too little; not too much.

In this place, no garden. Gussie, who generously cooks for me, insisted upon putting in a few inconspicuous cucumbers and squash and brought Lawrence, her husband, over to do the digging. This was last spring. I knew what would happen. I didn't tell her. She found out for herself. We have no deer here, but lashings of pheasant, woodchuck and various critters and I could just imagine them watching Gussie and Lawrence toil to clear a little space, giggling quietly to themselves, their bright eyes shining with anticipation.

There's a balance, always. I don't *need* a vegetable garden, pleasant as it is. (I do grow a little mint for iced tea, hard by the kitchen door.) After all, there's just me, with guests now and then or the children coming home to visit. It isn't the way it was on the bigger place with a couple of adults, four growing kids, their friends and the helpers in kitchen and garden. So, the farm down the road, where Gussie stops for eggs and corn, and the not-too-distant shining supermarkets meet our needs very well.

While I have been writing the clock has been creeping toward midnight and another day, so before I go up to bed I'll tear a sheet from the desk calendar.

Calendars are necessary; sidereal time is necessary; it is only practical to have it marked off for us in days, weeks, hours, minutes. But the true remembering, the valid rejoicing, the going forward toward the promise in which you believe isn't ruled by a calendar. It is of the heart and of the spirit. So our Easter rejoicing can be today or tomorrow or next week; and better still, always. . . .

Happy April!

A small altar

I have—as you knew I would—run out of fanciful, impossible architectural devices to lead us from one room and one month to another. But you can build an altar anywhere and a little chapel or temple to contain it; you can build it in your mind, and heart and spirit and take it with you.

To vow yourself daily upon this altar to God's will, no matter how often you fall short of your promise, is an exercise in faith. But never pledge yourself as a sacrifice. Most of us resent, whether unconsciously or not, having to sacrifice or be sacrificed. Rather, vow yourself as a gift, hoping to be acceptable and asking nothing in return.

I have often written and spoken of unanswered prayer and have said, as I believe, that prayer is always answered, even if not as we want it to be. When prayer appears to be unanswered in the way we have asked, it is because it is not God's will to give us something not according to His plan and purpose; and it occurred to me, quite recently that when despair closes in and prayer apparently goes unheard, it is not (as we are so apt to think) because God has failed us, but because we have failed God.

Prayer is an upward reaching. It can be achieved in long, solitary meditation, but also as you sit at a desk, or go to the office, or take a child to school or start the housework. There is no activity of mind and body which cannot be dedicated to God in a moment's time. There is nothing large or trivial which cannot be useful to Him, whether it is a great project, the work of one's mind, or cooking a good dinner.

I remember, almost always, to ask guidance in whatever I am undertaking, and especially if I believe I can help someone in sorrow or emergency. Recently a young friend of mine reminded me of a Quaker saying. I shall always remember it for it is quiet, beautiful and I am sure, powerful. I shall ask if someone needs me "to speak to his need."

Prayer is not a formalized spiritual act, even when we employ familiar and beautiful words; it is not restricted to church or even to the morning and evening at home; it is a tuning-in at any hour of the day and night, no matter what you are doing, or even saying to someone else, whether you are alone or with a number of people. It is a reaching to the Source, the limitless Source of help and guidance, supply, healing and love.

Prayer should be thankfulness, as well as petition. On a spring morning, be grateful; at the dawn of any lovely day and at its close. This, too, is prayer.

To pray for oneself is easy; to pray for those you love is even easier, but to pray for strangers and for your enemies—and often your enemy is yourself—that's harder. All of us pray for peace in a chaotic, confused world, not only our own peace but that of everyone, whether hostile or friendly. Many of us pray for all governments and the heads of governments and for spiritual enlightenment for all men. More and more, I think, despite the cry that the world is increasingly materialistic, people are beginning to understand the need for spiritual enlightenment—which will eventually mean what we call brotherhood. If one man experiences it, another will become aware. The impact of mind on mind, the influence of spirit on spirit—these are far greater, I am sure, than we know.

Certainly, in this sense we are our brothers' keepers, each of us a link in a chain. When a link weakens and breaks, we are all the poorer for it. Each man's failure reflects upon us all, whether he is friend or stranger; each of our own failures affects others than ourselves.

It is hard to face the fact of yourself, to grow older, look back and with a dreadful clarity see your mistakes. For some time now people have been blaming their errors and failures, deficiencies and troubles upon their parents, upon remembered insecurity, a lack of love, wrong guidance. It is certain that our adult lives are colored for good or evil by the attitudes of childhood, but I don't think anyone has ever said that we cannot outgrow attitudes, forgive the mistakes of others, and go forward. You can't put all the responsibility upon an indifferent mother, a harsh father, a broken home, a preferred brother or sister—no, not on any one of the hundreds of factors implicit in the complexities of family relationships. Now and then I read an autobiography in which the writer blames no one for anything which later happened to him; and there are even a few who say they had wonderful parents, a wonderful childhood and adolescence. These are rather rare because, of course, they do not make as sensational reading.

Most people can, if they think about it, find some flaws in their early years and those who do not publicly discuss them have my gratitude and admiration. It is, supposably, good therapy to Tell All on the printed page, as, we are informed, it gets it out of the writers' systems. I'm not so sure of that.

Whatever our parents did, or didn't do, they gave us life. And however responsible they were for frustrations, inhibitions and all the rest, we need not rest upon our oars and go drifting down the current toward the rocks or whirlpool. Maybe the oars they gave us weren't very strong, but they'll suffice if we learn to row.

We are responsible for ourselves. I doubt very much if we can justify making our heredity, environment and early relationships a blanket excuse for failure. Certainly the justice of God will take all the difficulties into account, yet hold us also responsible, for we are given mind, and spirit, and a free will.

We're like a piece of clay actually; in childhood so malleable. Perhaps through another's mistakes we become misshapen. But that can be corrected by the adult which the child becomes.

So on the little altar of the heart, mind and spirit let us vow to reshape ourselves into something closer to His image.

May

Now that it's May, I've hung a basket at the door. I'm always hanging things on the door, and this year it pleased me to renew my remembrance of May baskets; I haven't had one for many years. Ideally someone should have stolen silently up to the house before dawn and hung it for me. But, like everything else in life, if someone doesn't do it for you, try doing it for yourself.

When I was a child, I remember my parents taking me to visit friends who lived in the country and who adhered to this charming custom. I remember, too, that the place where we spent summers, and sometimes weekends, abounded in spring arbutus. In later years a friend in another state, where it was legal to pick it, used to send me some done up in wet moss and paper in a round, tin can. Nothing was ever sweeter.

This modern May basket of mine is small, but has a silver lining—well, tin at any rate—so I can keep the flowers in it for a time.

I always leave my many-colored ears of corn at the door longer than most people do and twice Gussie has discovered the doorstep pumpkins frozen (or eaten away by silent, little animals in the night) before she could make them into pies. I leave the Christmas wreaths up until Easter. This is not as odd as it sounds; I do not use glitter or artificial berries, just fresh pine with the small cones on the branches; all I have to do after the Christmas season is take off the red ribbon and the wreaths remain as a welcome. It's pleasant to come through a green-decked doorway in winter.

People deride or are indifferent to tradition nowadays. Old customs are difficult to maintain, I admit—the Yule log, for instance, for few have enormous fireplaces now. Maybe I'm a reactionary, but I like tradition. I'm not bound to it by chains of obligation or duty, or even nostalgia. I just like it, that's all.

I know that every month brings someone's birthday, so let me see who celebrates what, according to the record.

My sister's wedding anniversary is the tenth (and was it ever hot the day she was married!). My father was born in China (which isn't as far away now as it was then), on the twenty-first. My sister's youngest son, who died in Korea, was born May thirteenth, and her only daughter on the seventeenth. Oh, and my cousin Jessie on the second and my grandson Stephen on the twenty-ninth. That means CARE packages, and flowers in church for those no longer on this earth, and a scurrying about for birthday gifts for those who are.

On May days you can serve hot tea or iced. And how about bread and honey? May, to my mind, is as practical as bread and as sweet as honey.

Look at the birds. They've invested in their spring clothes, and building material and are occupied—those who didn't build earlier—with the manufacture of nests. Long since, I put scraps of bright yarn on the branches and bushes for those who built or rented earlier. Some of them are not inclined toward my taste in decoration, the blues and violets, the mauves and dusty pinks. A few are attracted to red and yellow, but most of them settle for the sober colors which do not clash with the shell tints of any egg.

I hope the orioles will return this year. They did last;
my daughter saw them, but I didn't; not on this property; not even one. Well, you can't have everything
even in May.

The leaves are as young as a baby in an incubator.
The grass will soon need cutting. The sky is a special
shade of blue and the rain, when it falls, is straight, gentle and warm. There'll be a new moon, there may be
high tides and there are such things as spring thunderstorms. I remember one May day when, suddenly, it
hailed.

It can be very warm this month; and occasionally
wool-suit weather. I remember a May evening, when,
driving back from the city after a personal ordeal, I
stopped for dinner off the Parkway and then went to
church where I quietly melted in the pew.

Lilacs are for May, and dogwood. I suspect that May
and October are my true loves—the one burning into
autumn, the other a jade-cool freshness before the summer's heat and dust.

After the May rains and little winds, the apple blossoms start to scatter. We have some old trees, and the
fruit they bear—if any—is not good, so I go out and
cut the branches and bring them into the house for
forcing. I never disturb the dogwoods. They don't like
it. And now the lilacs smell as the entrance to heaven
must. I bring these indoors, too—it's the best way to

prune them—but not too early. At the other place I had over forty bushes, all kinds; here, but a few, therefore all the more treasured. Incidentally, my sister and I drove around the old property on a springish day last winter. The house, its buildings and pool, together with some land, have been sold; the rest of the acreage is being developed and it gave me an odd feeling but brought no regret.

This is the month of gnats or midges or whatever you call them. What I call them I won't repeat. When I go outdoors on a soft spring evening, I pay if I don't tie a scarf around my head. They must have ancient Indian blood, the gnats, for they're always after my scalp.

Remember, when I spoke of the wasps last month? They have certainly had a marvelous hibernation in the attic, for there are masses of them. I don't know how they get down from the attic. The ceiling-door is closed except when we have to go up. It's all I can do to ascend and descend the ladder, but then I haven't wings.

I have never been a heroine, yet I have the proud distinction of being the only member of my family with the ability to attack the wasps, unafraid. I do not like to encounter them outdoors, for I'm not sure of what they're thinking, or thinking of *doing*. But in the house I am fearless. I bat them to the floor with a fly swatter or pluck them off a window in a piece of tissue.

Nothing is perfect, really, and that's just as well. If all

were perfection, how monotonous! Not that I enjoy irritations, such as midges; but there are more petty annoyances than those; everyone has his own special brand. One of mine is spring cleaning, especially when I know the house should be painted (inside and out) and I can't afford it; and when I remember that the last of the winter clothes must be safely put away and the summer cottons brought downstairs. Why is it that dresses seem to lengthen during their storage period, if the hems are to be worn shorter, or to grow shorter if the manufacturers decide we should let down our skirts?

The other day I made a mental list of the things which annoy me. They are like the May midges arriving without warning, practically invisible, to administer a sharp, brief sting and depart. If you're extra allergic, they leave a residual bump and itch.

On any day, in any month, I am irritated by any necessity to hurry. I'm irritated if the taxi's late. I'm anxious if the dinner guests are (there's a difference). I'm annoyed when I have to listen to a long-winded speaker (I'm one myself), and if there are discussions in my house or any other which blow up into arguments. (There's a difference there also.) Gaping clothes-closet doors or an open bureau drawer will get me out of bed to shut them. I can't stand finger marks on doors. Some summers ago, Gladys Taber introduced me to the dull horror of finger marks on light switches and thus added to my burden. I'd never noticed them before. Now I'm as alert as an airplane watcher.

Oh, very small complaints, but when several come along during a day, they add up, increasing the tension which seems normal for most of us. If, then, on the way to bed, I lose a slipper or stub my toe, or later have to answer a telephone which wakes me from my first sleep, I really feel martyred.

Everyone has a list of personal annoyances, whether it's kids tracking winter snow or spring mud into the newly scrubbed kitchen (and I don't care how often the advertising says it's of no importance, if you just whoosh it away) or the seller of something who comes to the door when you're busiest.

No one has been able to explain to me why I am so happy with the sound of running water, a brook, a waterfall, the drumming waves, the quiet whisper of a river on the shore, yet practically fly out of my skin if a faucet drips somewhere in the house. No one has informed me why the night sounds of small animals or the hooting of an owl pleases me, whereas if a dog barks at the moon, or howls interminably when his folks are away (as one across the road is doing at this moment), I am ready to throw the nearest and heaviest object. And that goes for battling or amorous cats, too.

Well, there are remedies. I can veil myself from

midges or, if they get me anyway, put something on the sting. The taxi will come, and if I'm late to an appointment, I'll apologize. If guests arrive an hour after the one fixed upon, we can keep dinner hot, hope for the best and not let their welcome be marred by an uneasy hostess. I can always close doors and bureau drawers, wash off the finger marks, polish the light switches and philosophically tell myself that when the winter clothes are bedded down, we're in a season free from snow. Yet, an almanac informs me that once, in this very section, a great many years ago, it snowed in July!

I'm sure it's possible to discipline oneself to take the minor upsets in stride. After all, they are unimportant; you have not experienced a loss, a blow, a catastrophe. This is a reasonable, philosophical point of view. But as one grows older, the trivialities seem larger. Still by now I should have more stoicism and common sense. I honestly believe I'm a little bit better than I was last year.

"Oh," people say to me, in person and by letter, "what a lovely, quiet life you lead, shut away in your study, walking down to the brook, seeing friends when you want to, the children grown and no longer responsibilities, the house hushed and your time your own for your work and play."

There's absolutely no answer to make except "Yes." You can't be with a stranger long enough to explain, face to face or by correspondence, that your time is never wholly your own, that grown children are still your children, and their anxieties yours; that you have obligations away from the desk and the house and that, once at the desk, work doesn't always come easily; often, the tide goes out and doesn't come in again for quite a spell.

In the ordinary sense, no one's time is fully his own, it belongs to the Musts—the duties and responsibilities. I suppose there are people who are exceptions to this rule, but I've never met them.

Yet, in the larger view time is our own. It is all eternity. It is what God has given us. We hurry through, we waste and squander and misspend it; we want what has gone returned to us, we demand benevolences from the future and consideration in the present.

All tenses being truly one, as the past has shaped us (that is to say, as we have shaped the past), so also the present is shaping us and the future will also. What is vital is how we meet time, what we do with it, and what it does to us because of our attitudes.

At this season of the year, if you don't hurry, if you forget about time, driving through the countryside and New England towns is an enduring joy. Recently, I saw apple blossoms blowing through an orchard; they looked like fragile snow and called to mind a day last December when the winds were gale high and delicate flakes blew horizontally, reminding me then of apple blossoms. It's easy to transfer yourself from season to season.

In spring, I like to take back roads—if the friend who drives me doesn't mind—and look into people's yards. Bulb gardens, magnolias—the late ones now—dogwood, lilac and flowering fruit trees. All these we can see as we drive. I also like to watch the activities in marinas and boat yards. These are the weekends when the men and boys of numberless households go to work on their boats; to scrape, and paint and put them ship shape again, ready, perhaps, by next weekend to slide into the blue, still-chilly waters of the Sound. This is happening all over the country in the spring, where there is water, where there are boats. And on the big highways, running through seemingly waterless country, I have seen canoes on the tops of cars, larger boats being towed in trailers, as their owners head for lakes and little rivers.

I was brought up boat-conscious. My father always had boats. He loved to sail, as well as take the wheel of a speed or fishing boat. I knew all the waters around us, the Sound, Peconic Bay, and in later years something of the St. Lawrence where I spent a month each summer. Nowadays my yachting, so to speak, has been confined to watching boats when I'm on Cape Cod, or going on a day's fishing trip, or admiring the way Gladys Taber paddles a canoe. When I'm on Long Island with my sister, I can at least see boats, and last summer I had two days of deep-sea fishing in the Bay of Fundy.

Now, in the bright May weather, I am hoping that some of my friends who own big boats or little, will take me out upon the shining waters, to sail, or to fish. I haven't set foot on a deck since the Bay of Fundy experience, when my daughter and I went out with wonderful people in a fishing craft; we went twice in fog, in chill and rain. We loved it. We also loved reaching Nova Scotia via a long ferry crossing from Bar Harbor to Yarmouth and later, the shorter passage from Digby to St. John. Fog on both these trips, too, but we didn't care.

Boats, little or big, have to be cared for, whether you call them boats, cruisers or yachts. They have to have their sparkle renewed, their sails mended or replaced, their motors tuned up and their barnacles removed.

Barnacles are living things and inimical to man. They cluster grimly about piers. I once cut my foot getting off a dock into the water and swam the half mile I was projecting, conscious that I hurt. I still bear the scar. Barnacles attach themselves to living creatures, also. There is a story told about the Kona coast of the Island of Hawaii, in which it is said that every year a very old shark swims to a certain place where he is met by a Japanese fisherman who waits till the shark rears up out of the water and then scrapes the barnacles from his poor old back. No member of the fisherman's family, so the tale goes, has ever been harmed by a shark.

This story was told to me, and others, by a friend who has a place on that coast and knows the fisherman. The day after I heard it, I spoke to the little Japanese woman who was manicuring my nails in the beauty salon of the hotel where we were staying. And all she said was, "Of course, he's a member of the Shark family!"

As far as I know barnacles serve no good purpose. They are crustaceans, but I doubt that anyone eats them. That statement may bring me an avalanche of mail from people who love them for breakfast, so I shall amend it by saying, I've never heard of anyone eating them.

Watching the scraping activities at a marina the other late afternoon I began to think of people as ships. It's hardly a new thought; thousands have had it before me. But surely, we are fashioned by the Master Builder and launched into this world, wherein for a brief time we live. Our experiences and environments, our thinking and attitudes combine to produce the currents and crosscurrents, the shoals and reefs; they cry up the storms and make the winds to rise; they bring us the landfall and harbors as well. I often dream about harbors, safe harbors, and their lights—symbolic of home, but mainly of love, which is the only true security.

Barnacles abound upon every human ship—hate and resentment, anger and prejudice, envy and unkindness —and a ship infested with barnacles doesn't sail very well.

To identify oneself with a small boat—and who'd have the temerity to deem himself a yacht or an ocean-going liner?—is a little frightening. How do we know what storms we must encounter, what winds will fill the sails or which trouble silence the engines?

How do we know that, having set our course for a certain port, we'll reach it or whether or not we'll see the harbor lights? How do we know what difficulties will beset us or what rocks are hidden beneath the dark waters?

We don't. But there's enormous comfort in trust. This is the life preserver.

The Master Builder is also the Maker of Charts, and we can trust the course He has planned. To be sure we must do much of our own steering, and we often stray perversely from the course. But the waters of life beneath, the sky above and the stars we steer by are all manifestations of God.

May is a happy month. Be happy in it; and grateful for time and spring.

The patio

This morning, as I sat down at the typewriter, I suddenly remembered a house in Palm Springs where, in order to reach one of the bedrooms, you had to cross a patio from the porch—or as they say, in Hawaii, *lanai*. So now I'm back designing things again.

Therefore we will enter June by crossing a low-walled patio. Beyond the one of which I am thinking there is grass and a fountain; and, of course, all manner of growing things, but I can replan it for my own purposes.

A patio, by whatever name you call it—it's terrace, in other places, I suppose—is a sort of interlude . . . it is a part of the pattern of the house, yet it's a unit in itself. It is planned for rest, for sunlight, for descending dusk, for looking up and away, and as night deepens, for regarding the immensity of stars. From the Palm Springs patio you have a view. You look to the desert with its muted shades of gray green and dusty yellow; and to the mountains, where for a large part of the year there is snow on the highest peaks.

From a patio like this, the hours bring a procession of wonders. Sunset is early here. The sun drops behind the mountains and dusk is upon them, a dusk tinted with rose and gold, mauve and blue. But because it is early, you know that behind the distant peaks the sun still shines.

At night, the mountains are darker shapes against darkness; if there is snow, there is a frosty glittering of stars, and if there is moonlight, on desert and mountain, you are confronted with an unearthly beauty.

Let us add to the house through which we move— not only the house of the year but the house of our personal life—such a structure. We can build it from many materials: hope and dreams and remembering, but mostly, I think, prayer.

To emerge from the confusion and tension of everyday living into the desired quietude of a place of our own—warmth when we need it, coolness when it is most necessary—is restoration. Here is sanctuary, but without high walls. It is a cloister wherein we can be silent and meditate and derive new strength and enduring courage.

The desert is not barren. It blooms in spring and year around it offers little marvels. The mountains are not barriers; they are pathways to the stars. The quiet is not lonely. You have never been more companioned than in such a silence.

When a day begins which you know will be difficult, or one ends which has been, take time to walk from the room which people invade, in which telephones ring, and apprehensions wait in corners. Go into the patio and stay awhile, looking out and away—looking up, and asking for whatever you need, but promising to work toward it. Shelter yourself behind its low walls. Little walls shelter you, yet do not shut you out from anything important.

It is vital to the human mind, body and spirit to know periods of solitude. These are not often achieved physically, but there can be, in brief moments, a withdrawal, mentally and spiritually, for refreshment and restoration.

Look out; look, always, up; as a wonderful man said

recently in my hearing, "If God had meant you to look down, your eyes would be in your feet."

So now, cross the patio, with me, from May into June.

June

June is the traditional month of brides who are almost certain to be surrounded by scented clouds of blowing white. The lilacs have gone, the magnolias, the dogwood, but the pink and white flowering bushes are still in bloom and the roses busily climbing everywhere. This is a sweet season, the trees not yet burdened with heavy foliage or dust, and the birds still preoccupied with domesticity. Yet any month belongs to the bride. I remember a January bride who looked like June incarnate—very young, small and blonde. I remember better still a November bride who looked through the windows of her parents' home upon a dull, dark, threatening day and saw only sunlight. And only last December I almost froze to death watching a white-gowned girl get out of a car and go into her church. It was subfreezing weather, but in her heart I am sure it was June.

June isn't always blue and gold and brilliant. She has all sorts of tricks up her flowing green sleeves. Sometimes she's mischievous, bringing cold wet days. I recall the time I planned an outdoor picnic for a woman's service club which had made me an honorary member during the previous winter. I was all set with extra help, long tables in the yard, chairs on the grass and terrace and a barbecue broiler. It was a weekday and as the members, who are businesswomen, gathered on the terrace and in the yard after work, it began to rain, and went right on raining. This is not a house geared for thirty or more people at a buffet, but we managed, thanks to Gussie, Lawrence and the amiable flexibility of my guests.

June seems to present us with almost as many obligations as December. (What month does not?) In the birthday department this month marks the anniversaries of two close friends now absent from this plane of living; the birthday of one up north and that of a dearly beloved daughter-in-law.

There are also a wedding and graduations, which call for shopping and attendance. I don't go to many weddings, or graduations, either, but there are always the exceptions. Not too long ago I went to the first high-school graduation I'd witnessed in years to watch a tall boy, whom I'd known since his childhood, get his diploma. Last June I flew to Michigan to talk at the first graduation exercises of a country day school for girls. It was hotter than the seven hinges of you-know-where, and the parents wilted: the papas in their collars, ties and jackets; the mamas in their pretty frocks and hats, to say nothing of the headmistress and teachers in gowns and mortarboards, and the graduates in white.

I did not wear cap and gown, since I had never earned them. So I could not march in the academic procession but went alone to the rostrum where I sat at the end of a choir pew and cowered until it came my turn.

When I rose to speak I realized that I'd never felt as inadequate. What do you tell eighteen-year-olds? How warn, and how encourage?

I am, so to speak, on the homestretch; what could I offer to those just starting to run the course? How I envy the many speakers (on all subjects) whom I have heard, so certain of their own wisdom and infallibility. I don't know *anything* really, save what I've learned from my own experience and even that I see through a glass darkly—tinted as it is with hindsight and with my own excuses for myself—so, really, I haven't learned very much; except that I'm nearer ignorance than wisdom.

Quite a while ago I was a little astonished when the sons and daughters of my contemporaries began rushing to the altar and the invitations flooded in. Then the children of friends younger than myself decided upon the Big Leap. Just the other day it horrendously occurred to me that any year now I'll have invitations from my contemporaries' children, bidding me to the weddings of *their* children. My own grandchildren will not be of marriageable age for some time, thank heaven, although the two oldest, being girls, could, if they put their minds to it, manage in a decade or even less.

Practially every chapter I write contains the same unanswered inquiry: What happens to Time and what is Time anway?

Remembering with a hard, brilliant clarity something that happened thirty-five or forty years ago, but forgetting your own telephone number, is not necessarily a symptom of advanced senility. It's sometimes merely the sudden timelessness of time, which is rather like an accordian—or as one of my children used to say of his brother's favorite instrument, "squeeze box"—drawing out, collapsing, coming together again.

One thing I could have told those very young graduates last year—but didn't and wouldn't—was that the loneliness most of them experience during adolescence will stay with them all of their earthly lives. I do not mean those seizures of loneliness which overtake any of us, at any age and at any time, because we think we are misunderstood, or we feel rejected, or because people we love fail to meet us—or we to meet them—on a mutual mental or emotional plane. Nor do I mean the physical loneliness of the withdrawn person—and there are many—who, as we say, "has no one," who doesn't make friends easily and, doesn't basically want to, being afraid of being hurt. And I certainly don't mean the isolated moments, usually at plane or train or automobile time, when, restless and sometimes anxious, we wait for someone—a little overdue—to return home.

No. This life-lasting loneliness is not of mind or body or emotions; it's been experienced by almost everyone who has ever lived, from physical childhood through physical maturity into physical old age. It can be known by people securely and warmly surrounded by love: those who have husbands or wives, children, grandchildren, hundreds of friends and acquaintances; by those with parents, sisters and brothers, and those who have no difficulty whatsoever in meeting strangers. It can be felt by people who are working in some supremely satisfactory profession or position. It has nothing whatever to do with the so-called status, the houses lived in, the things money buys, or even the things we haven't enough money to buy.

I have often spoken of the rare, sudden flashes of pure joy, not outwardly caused; joy without, as it were, any reason and said I believed it to be of the spirit. The special loneliness, which makes itself felt, also infrequently is, I think, of the spirit which, caged in the demanding, active, experiencing flesh, must at times be not only lonely but homesick.

Perhaps when the earth is locked in the iron, icy embrace of winter, she longs for spring, for June, for blossoming, always knowing that, in time, it will come, being inevitable, and that always, even under the frozen soil, growth is waiting. Comprehending this, the longing becomes but a brief impatience. So can the spirit be less lonely, realizing that no matter what outwardly happens, there is growth, spring after winter, sun after snow, blossom after rain. So can a little spiritual loneliness be good for all of us.

I spoke of this loneliness the other day to a friend, who misinterpreted what I said. She murmured sympathetically, "You must be depressed." But I wasn't. (Words are such barriers; everyone knows their dictionary meaning but each also reads his own significance into them.)

Everyone is at times depressed, and by varying causes . . . discouraged, burdened with the sense of failure, uneasy under what we think of as too much responsibility. Anyone with any sensitivity at all suffers with his friends' losses and difficulties, and there are certainly days during which nothing goes right from job—whether household, office or both—to the many human relationships. On such days the postman brings no news other than that of disappointment, disaster or crisis, and even the telephone has an eerie, warning sort of ring. So certainly we're depressed and small wonder! But the spiritual loneliness of which I speak is not a reaction to anything done, or heard, or even feared.

Believing, as I do, that the human spirit is a part of the great creative Spirit of God, I think that, now and again, the awareness of loneliness is the spirit's realization of its unity with the Creator, Who made us, the earth and seas, the sky, the planets and stars in their orbits and on their courses.

Nowadays everyone speaks most casually of the orbits in which the man-made satellites travel willy-nilly, aiming at the innocent moon, or leonine sun, with failure or success. I feel ignorant and abashed because I know so little, and if all this were explained to me, I'd probably not understand it any better than I do that international date line. But the other day I looked up *orbit* in my two-volume Oxford dictionary (abridged, it says here, the unabridged one must be incredible) and found out when the word came into the language. In astronomy "orbit" has been used for a very long time and, since 1759, also in a figurative sense.

We often speak of a person as being "out of his orbit" or "coming into" somebody else's, by which we mean "sphere of influence"; we speak of people "changing" their orbits, that is to say either expanding or narrowing them. And we are, of course, referring to position in life, to occupations, interests, to progressing or regressing, as the case may be. How many of us, I wonder, reflect at all upon the spiritual orbit?

Under the leafed-out June trees the ground is damp with dew and the stars wheel above, indifferent, silver, and exceedingly bright. Not too long from now, on the ninth of this month to be exact, the moon will be full. I wonder what the man in the moon thinks of satellites?

I have always been, like dogs and lunatics—and that word comes from *luna* or *moon*—afflicted by moonlight. When others cry that it is romantic (and so it is) and love watching it—often rising red, cooling to gold and paling to silver, filtering through the leaves to make a mysterious, achingly magic path upon the water— I, from childhood on, have regarded it with melancholy. To this day, I didn't know why. One of my girl children has inherited this lamentable trait and she doesn't know why, either. I remember particularly a moon which was full, late in another June, and which seemed to me the loveliest manifestation of nature I'd ever seen; yet, even then the fatal flaw to complete enjoyment was apparent, the foreboding, the melancholy.

Is it possible that from childhood I forswore the moon, regarding her with a singular misery because somehow I knew that, over half a century later, she would rise above the trees and look down at me, perhaps with pity?

Is she a dead world, an empty crater, reflecting the sun? What is she, really? I often wonder, but have no desire to invade her and find out. It is enough for me to see her light and know her beauty, even though, in her presence, I feel unaccountably saddened.

The orbit in which man's spirit revolves is similarly afflicted, but by what we call the "gravitational pull," for surely the human mind and physical body draw the aspiring spirit downward. Only in the half moments of sudden, inexplicable splendor do we somehow escape and find ourselves breathing, however briefly, the breath of the immortal spirit of all mankind.

It is in vain that we pray to be spared the anxieties, the pressures and tensions of daily living; the overcrowded moments, the prodding of hurry, the awareness of failure, terror and regret. Asking to be spared them is a child's prayer: "Don't let it rain on the picnic." For all these things are part of normal living and anyone who loves anyone else in whatever relationship must experience them all, and more; anyone who must make a living, maintain a house, plan a future and look back to a past, has to know these things. Only by laboring around and over them, as over and around any physical obstacle in our road, do we learn to conquer and to grow. But it's awfully hard sometimes. How often have you said to yourself: "If things aren't better soon, I'll throw in the towel"? I'm amazed if you've never thought that. I have time and time again. But the dark, hag-ridden night always becomes tomorrow's day.

A fresh start? Every day is, really. As I've said before, ignoring the calendar, a new year is just another day, but the calendar's artificial division makes it something seemingly more important. Last New Year's Day I said to someone, "Well the old year's gone, and this one must be better." And she said, "If it isn't, you have only three hundred and sixty-four—or is it three hundred and sixty-five in a Leap Year?—before the next new year comes!"

I do not think that the spirit marks the passage of time in its struggle to reach the orbit in which it was created to function, however often it fails because of the earth pull.

Surely, that orbit is limitless and beyond the knowledge of any human mind?

When I think of the manufactured satellites and even of those not created by man—the stars and planets, sun and moon—I try to think past them to the endless traveling, the long journey, of the spirit. For its true goal must be the course destined for it, the ceaseless revolution around the immeasurable light, love, compassion, power and glory which is God.

So when things are close to the verge of what we imagine is the unendurable; when the wall looms high and blank in front of us, so that we cannot see over or around or through it; when the path leads to what looks like a dead end; when nights are spent in vigil and prayer, and days in driving the tired body to manifold duties, we can endeavor to think of the spirit, struggling to rise above all this and know its own freedom and its true path. And, whether in January or June, we can listen for a voice which says: Be still and know that I am God.

Walk with me for a while under the young leaves which laugh a little in the wind, look up again at the sky. There are the timeless stars, pursuing their orderly courses.

But the grass grows damp, and the wind, a trifle chilly. So let us return to the house, switch on the lights, close the shutters, draw the pale rose curtains and sit for a while on the pink love seats and tell each other what is in our hearts, this June.

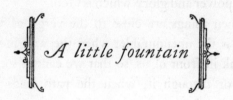

A little fountain

I'm back in the patio, I like it here. . . . In the actual one there's a fountain beyond, through the wrought-iron gates, but here I shall build my own. . . .

I think it's pink marble; I have a passion for pink marble. Some years ago I talked about a pink marble coffee table until close friends, tired of listening to me, gave me one for my birthday; a just-right one; the legs even matched the Phyfe-reproduction love seats. I am sorry to say that I walked into the house after a summer on Cape Cod and looked first at the curtains. I'd bought the material in the spring, and they'd just been hung for autumn and winter. I'd forgotten the design. While I was congratulating myself on them, my daughter said, "I wish you'd look down." I did so, and there was the coffee table. It fitted so perfectly into the surroundings I hadn't even seen it.

So, pink marble for the fountain and the rimmed pool into which it splashes. And for the smaller basin, or whatever you call it, that first catches the water, a sea shell, as lovely and intricate as a flower. And sea horses around the rim. I don't care if real sea horses *don't* come in pink!

There is nothing cooler-sounding than the quiet splashing of a fountain unless it's the conversation of a brook hurrying to its destination, in deep, still woods. But a fountain which sings close to a desert has a special serenity.

The desert is quiet, too, in the place of which I am thinking, except for the wind in the low growth and the scurrying of little animals, the delicate high stepping of quail. The desert is dust and sand and the struggle for survival. How courageous the desert flowers, creeping in color after a spring rain, the twisted ancient trees and the bushes which maintain their precarious root-hold! The desert has its own oases, of course, but here with a fountain speaking to it in the cool of the sunrise, and dusk, and the heat of the day, how encouraged it must feel!

There is a desert of the mind, when what we call inspiration fails—all creative workers know this—and when nothing grows, not even the stunted trees and bushes. Then it seems truly wasteland. You can almost feel the sand eroding the edges of thought. Either there's no wind at all, or an arid one blowing, and you wonder if you'll ever write or paint or carve again.

There is a desert of the heart, too; and this is the dwelling place of loss, of grief, of bereavement. The physical heart is strong and stubborn; it goes on beating, while the heart within the heart is more barren than the Sahara and there is no oasis.

But the mind's desert knows the sudden life-giving rain, the awakening of color and the wind of creative thought, and then it is no longer a desert but a garden. And the heart's desert, while it may never fully bloom again, knows the compassion of God, under which hope is revived and a desire to fulfill its mission and most of all, to accept.

Like the fountain, springing from far beneath the earth, a fountain unsealed, a fountain which is ever present, is the compassionate understanding of God who made the physical deserts, the oases and gardens.

In our everyday lives there are barren places, but there are also springs and streams and upwelling of cool

water. The Psalmist knew this when he said, "he lead-
eth me beside the still waters."

In every heart, mind and spirit there is a fountain
waiting. You can listen for it in the silence of the night
or in a crowded street. Rising, falling, singing of hope,
of gratitude and of peace.

"Golden peace," the Chinese say to one another.
. . . In golden peace, with the sound of a fountain
nearby, let us walk from June into July.

July

A good deal of mail comes to my desk and much of it asks me to describe this house, the place in which I live. July's a little too warm usually to take the tour down the slope and past the small brook-fed pool—which is often dry in July anyway—and so around through the fields and brambles, trees and back again.

However, it isn't hard to describe.

In most houses, during the summer, doors—if they're screened—stand open, literally. Figuratively, almost everyone's doors are open year 'round. When I meet someone, I often say, "Stop by." Not always, for everyone knows that there are people you wouldn't make happier—nor they, you—if they did.

If you should come to this house to visit with me for a while, you'd find, when you drive up, a little red barn (rather new—the old one fell down) and an old brick walk. At least the bricks are old; the walk we had laid when we moved some years ago. It splits two ways: one path goes to the kitchen and its roofed stone porch; the other, past a stone terrace to the side entrance. Remember we never use the front door. When I am home, summers, I have terrace boxes there, three of them, usually filled with pansies, pink geraniums and ivy—and on the kitchen porch a big stone urn of geraniums.

But now we are at the side door. If you look through the screen, as you approach, you may think there's a man standing there. There isn't. It is the portrait of my grandfather as a very young man which confronts you. It's too big for the miniature front entrance hall. Actually it belongs to my elder son, but he has lent it to me because I love it.

So there is Grandfather Baldwin opposite the door, and to the right of it there's an old mirror—about 1800—with the painted picture at the top; and I've some carved sea birds sitting on that. There's a round, small table and an old glass lamp with pattern-glass handles.

Its bayberry-decorated shade was painted on the Cape. On the rather beat-up table, under Grandfather's portrait, you will find the things I'm fond of seeing every day.

All year round there's an antique wooden tea caddy. Open it and you'll find zinc-lined compartments for the tea and an old sugar bowl. At Christmas I fill the bowl with holly; at Easter, I put a Victorian china egg in it—and leave the top of the caddy open. Sometimes, in summer, I put a few little branches of pine in it.

Always, too, there's a green-gray celadon Sung bowl, sometimes, as I've said, filled with gourds; sometimes holding a plant. And there are Copenhagen porcelain ornaments and, usually, a dark, etched vase full of flowers.

In summer, I like the appearance of coolness. So in July the flowers are white, or just the pine branches, and the figurines,—a pair of love birds, a Chinese dove, and maybe a dull green grasshopper.

If you will come into the living room and look through the big east window, you will immediately encounter an enormous mulberry tree, twisted, hurricaned, ice-stormed almost—but not quite—to death. It grows up past the second-story windows and is usually busy with birds and squirrels. The first year I moved here it bore fruit, and then no more until this summer.

Beyond that the slope, the line of tall pines to the right, the pond, and apple trees and maples.

The south window is even bigger; there's a bulb garden under it and some laurel bushes, and on a little rise the bird bath set in the ground and not quite plumb. It's an old millstone, and it couldn't be busier. The first summer I came here to live, I sat absolutely bemused at sunset, watching an oriole and a bluebird and a couple of goldfinches splashing around, and then flying up to preen in the bushes.

Always the pines and firs, the spruce and cedar, are green, and the deciduous trees, at this time of year, cut us off from a very unexpected view of Long Island Sound.

In July the living room wears its summer dress— pale peppermint-striped mint-green and sand-colored. The curtains blow white and much of the familiar clutter has been put away, although you'll still find a Kwan Yin, a green wine ewer and a lot of the old mugs I collect.

Unlike most collections, this one—Staffordshire, pattern glass, German, French, and Chinese luster and other ware—is used. The mugs, all shapes and sizes, hold cigarettes or flowers, and upstairs some of them are full of cotton balls to take the shine off feminine noses.

If you like tea, there will be, I hope, some mint—provided you like mint—and plenty of ice (which I don't use at all) lots of lemon and the hollow-stemmed Mexican silver spoons my sister brought me from Mexico.

This is a lazy month, knee-deep in summer, steeped in the scent of strawberries and hay and sun. We have wild strawberries here; I always see them at blossom time and scarcely ever find them when the fruit is ripe.

Vacations now. Ever since June people have been holidaying. Perhaps I'll get to Cape Cod sometime. I love it so much, but I also like coming home again.

Even when you aren't vacationing, summer seems to slow the blood and the pace. That's a good thing. If time, as they say, is money, and if I could only have back all the time I've wasted in hurrying, I'd be rich.

I lived in a city for many years, and we had a back yard. Houses with back yards are still there I suppose, but apartment buildings don't always have yards. Oh, some of course, have spaces which people can share and where young mothers wheel the babies, and watch the older children. For many city people escape is to a beach, however crowded, or on a few hours' ride to the hills. For those in villages and on farms there are woods and fields and time, in a long evening, to loaf and invite the soul. The shadows are long and golden, dusk comes late, long after supper. There are nights, rolling with thunder, crackling with the whiplash of lightning, nights crowded with stars and resplendent with the moon in any one of her lovely phases.

Living is a hurrying, exciting business. But I have learned in recent years to take a little time from the pace of living and just *live*.

In a lifetime, we live, it seems, a thousand years and as many lives, in a sense, for we are no more the same people we were half an hour ago than we'll be tomorrow. Growth is slow, almost imperceptible; you don't notice it from day to day. All experiences leave marks like grooves in a record; if you could play it back, how astonished you would be, how happy, how stricken, how ashamed and how proud.

It's wonderful to consider that, however preoccupied with ourselves and daily living, we share a common lot with every human being in this world, no matter where they are or what they are doing; whatever their environment, circumstances, race, creed or pigmentation. Fundamentally, we all have the same basic needs. They are easy to sum up: each of us must, in his own way, worship, love, work and play; all need food and shelter; each has been born and someday will die.

I have known many people more fortunate in their circumstances than others. But I have never known anyone at all who has not suffered grief or physical pain; who has not, at one time or another, been desperately anxious; or who has never experienced fear and frustration. Each in his own manner and at his appointed time.

To feel a kinship with the woman you meet when you're shopping, with the parents of other children, or another girl in love—if you happen to be—or with someone stabbed by sorrow (remembering your own) is easy. You can be aware of a likeness to others, in work, play and needs. But to know that you have—whether you like them or not, whether you never even meet them—a kinship with everyone in this world can be a wonderful awareness.

To each one his personal sorrow or problem seems unique, and, indeed it is, because no two people are exactly alike or feel any emotion in precisely the same way. But, the underlying likeness is still there.

There is another need, too, as necessary as bread. And that is the need to be needed; to be useful to someone, whether one person or many.

People often say, "No one needs me."

Those who speak so are the hurt and lonely, yet they have only to open their eyes and their hearts, go out and seek. They will find that many people will need them.

And God needs us, as we need Him. Think of it in this way—the child needing his parent, the parent needing his child.

I do not believe—and have often said so—that one human soul is more valuable to God than another. Certainly many are evolved beyond others, and hence more valuable to humanity. But to God, I am certain that each human spirit, following its own difficult path—which, no matter what one does to himself, always leads upward—is equally valuable.

Here, too, is kinship and wonder, the sense of being useful and wanted.

People look alike, talk alike, think alike—or so we say. I was thinking about this last winter during a snowstorm and I remembered that it is said no two flakes are the same. I, somehow, cannot grasp this. All over the visible world snow has been falling where, in season, one can expect it, for as many years as the earth's existence. So much snow that the mind reels contemplating it; and yet no two flakes are exactly the same.

Nor is one July exactly like past Julys, in hourly temperatures, humidity readings, storm patterns and events. That goes for the other eleven months, too.

Inanimate objects can be alike—apparently. For instance, the houses in a development structurally speaking, but what about the insides of those houses? Furniture can come off an assembly line like cars—one chair as like another as cars of the same make and model.

But if a thousand people buy that same model chair or car, there is change: differences in wear, usage, care or abuse.

No sorrow is, line for bitter line, like another; the basic cause may be the same, but the grief is personal to him who grieves.

Several of us were talking the other night about the changes which have come to the countryside about us and the villages in which we live—some for all our lives so far, others for twenty or more years—and I remarked that the youngsters of today would, in twenty years, exclaim over the way *their* villages had changed.

In this world, moment by moment, there is alteration in everything. You do not see it, but it's there; or perhaps you do see it, suddenly, as I did when they began to build a school in back of me, where there were fields, not long ago. When I moved here, there were no street lights on my road. Recently someone has sent me a clipping which announces that there will be, very soon.

I have fields, and no one builds on them, but they, too, are altering—not alone the trees and undergrowth but the soil. As for the vacant lot not far from me, it just sits there happily, but somewhere there's a potential buyer, a builder with the beginning of a plan in his mind. He just hasn't happened along yet. But he will.

I look now across the smallest hall in the world—
just a place where you take off for the first step upstairs—and there's the dining room. I can't, from
here, see the corner cupboard with the Chinese things,
but I know they are there. The Ming Kwan Yin is old,
but she looks exactly as she did when she was given to
me. But how do I know what alterations are invisibly
taking place within the atoms which compose her com-
posure?

As I said earlier, we aren't as we were half an hour
ago. I'm not the same person that I was when I sat
down to write this. I am, for instance, a little older and
what I am thinking is making little etchings in my
brain, or so I've been told. From moment to moment
the pattern changes.

We do not live in a static world—physically or emo-
tionally, mentally or spiritually. When I think of the
spectacular advances and alterations I myself have witnessed in science, medicine, architecture, the arts and
in people's thinking, since my birth, I am amazed. Also,
I am happy to have lived in this era. Some of us—I'm
one—may not like it wholly. But all must agree it's
been interesting.

All of which reminds me of July's birthdays; that of
my friend Agnes, of my older daughter and her
younger child. It's the birth month of a friend in Nevada and of my publisher in New York. And the

thirtieth is the birthday of a very close friend who just won't stay home so we can celebrate it with her. Well, she did once. Maybe she will this month and we'll have a picnic.

Picnics have become more civilized than when I used to have them in a city back yard, in public parks or on beaches with my children. Now places are provided where you can cook and tables at which to eat, and ants must grow discouraged.

When I think of picnics, I dream of Cape Cod and of sheltering under the dunes or down by the Mill Pond, and of watching from Nauset Beach the waves cream over the sands. Then, of course, I think of Gladys and Eleanor whose house has always been open to me.

Eleanor went away last January, but so strong was the impact of this gentle, quiet, rock-firm, understanding woman upon everyone who knew her that, for us, she has just gone next door. We are the poorer for her going; Heaven, the richer. And nothing is ever really lost, no valid friendship and love.

Now the fireflies are out. Did you know just one can light a dark room? In New Zealand, their sister glowworms illuminate for twenty-four hours a day a vast cave arching over an underground river.

When I moved to the first country house, it was mid-June and hot and as there were no screens, the fireflies came in. They could have been, as the friend with me said, men carrying lanterns. One Sunday, last winter, my clergyman spoke of small lights; each of us can be one, he reminded us. Shakespeare said that, too, in another way.

Often I have friends here, or go out for a pleasant evening, and then, to bed, when the door's shut and locked, when the good-byes have been said. I am drowsy and happy, but if, before I sleep, I review the day past, I grow discouraged casting up the accounts. So far, I'm in the red. And I've been wondering since last winter how often I exhibit the tiny light? Very seldom, I'm afraid. And by "light" I don't mean platitudinous preachments or the sort of sticky sweetness some people exude. I just mean the ordinary courtesies, like listening—and not interrupting. I mean the effort not to hurt people, even unintentionally; not contributing to what we call "harmless" gossip, and not thinking or talking after the usual negative fashion.

To be a light in a dark room all the time, how wonderful that would be! I doubt if many human beings have succeeded in consistently producing from within the light which is as the tiniest taper taking fire from the illumination which is God—the light of quietude and forbearance, justice and compassion, and patient, intelligent love.

So many things serve to quench the light, for a long

time, or momentarily: despair, disillusion, cynicism, the knowledge of our own shortcomings and the disloyalties or treacheries of others. Self-pity puts the light out; frustration and envy, resentment and evasion, prejudice and self-deception—these are all snuffers.

But the light can be rekindled. In few of us does it go out for good. In fact, I don't believe it *ever* quite goes out. I believe it is always trying to manifest, even as a spark.

Where will I be this July? Maybe on Long Island with my sister, walking by the enormous pond and looking across the sand bar to the sea or at her garden, her wonderful roses. Perhaps I'll be on the Cape, sooner or later, looking at a long white beach or timidly venturing into the Mill Pond. I don't care what any of its devotees say, this water which comes from the Atlantic via a couple of inlets is always colder than January.

July is a skyrocketing month. On the Fourth I cower quietly in a back room for, law or no law, people set off anything from torpedos to what sounds like guided missiles—and I hate noise.

I'm also terrified of thunderstorms—not of being struck by lightning, for how I depart this life is of no moment to me as long as I don't make it hard for other people—but I'm plain, downright scared of fire. This old house is built of wood and when the lightning gallops and thunder crashes, I remember I'm a long way from a fire department and there isn't a hydrant within walking distance.

I wonder what I'd try to save beside myself and any-one else in the house—although usually there isn't any-one in it but me, nights—if a bolt came whooshing through.

Well, you expect July to be July. When you look at the trees, the fireflies, the roses dreaming of dew, you accept them. Looking out at the myriad birds I think how kind they are to nest awhile near me, bring up their young, use the bird bath, sit on the feeders and sing. You expect birds in July—even though most of them vanish at midday—but not in January. Then there is nothing to equal the sight of a cardinal flaming on a bare branch above the snow or a dove mincing around the frozen water in the millstone.

In January every bird is a gift—the unexpected tow-hee, the pheasant, the bluebird (we had some here, at Christmas), the nun-coiffed junco; every nuthatch and titmouse and chickadee, and, of course, the firebird.

For it's always the beauty you don't expect which pierces your heart. In July there's fulfillment and ev-erything teems about you, but in stark January the bright red bird is a gift from God. He truly is.

Slipping as we do from season to season, we rarely

stop to think, not only of the wonders of the present but of the joy of events past, the promise of the future. Great minds have said, "Live now, live today—it's only the Now you really know."

They are right, in the over-all pattern, but I like to look back a little, and a little ahead. I don't neglect, despise or discount what's happening this very minute, but for me to live in the exact moment is impossible. Which proves I don't have a great mind. In a way, I'm glad, for it would be both a burden and a responsibility. I like being very much like everyone else; otherwise I'd understand them only from the intellectual and psychological viewpoint.

Wisdom is a bird's-eye view. Mine's a worm's-eye, I suppose—very close to the ground and seeing the average person much as the average person sees me.

Whatever July brings, it won't matter as long as I'm with people I love and can look upon beauty.

This to me is a wonderful world. It is so small in comparison with the universe; just a pinprick in the cosmic pattern, but wonderful. I feel privileged, no matter what has happened, is happening or will happen, to have lived in it for a good many years—and grateful.

Joyous vacation, picnics, parties, home-coming and July—the golden heart of summer.

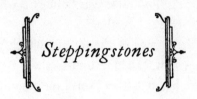

Steppingstones

It is pleasant to have a free hand in building, without blueprint and scale maps or any material but thought and imagination. The patio as an entrance to another room still appeals to me. But now I've redesigned it as a terrace.

There is no longer a desert and mountain view; this terrace is tree-shaded, and in one corner is built right round a tree. Don't think you can't do this. My father's house on Shelter Island was an old farmhouse when he bought it. He made several additions, the first being a one-story dining room. Then a pantry and kitchen with rooms above it. The builder planned to run a porch across the front of the dining room, but there was a great tree in the way. "Build around it," my father said in his lordly fashion. So it was done and with plenty of room for the tree to breathe.

Now in the corner of the terrace which you cross to get into a room called August, there's a tree, two lounge chairs beneath it and small metal tables.

There are steps going down to a wide, smooth lawn and on the edge of it, between the manicured grass and the meadow I think I'll have a brook so we can listen to it awhile but mainly in order to have steppingstones.

We'll widen the path, right there. No bridge—we've been on a bridge—just big, variously shaped stepping-stones.

As I have explained, I'm normally unsteady, and to get from one actual stone to another affords me considerable apprehension. But I am fond of steppingstones, just as I am of old-fashioned fences with stiles in them.

Perhaps I told you my sister took many pictures on her trip to the Orient. As she is a garden-buff, a majority of them are of gardens: a moss garden and those gardens with tiny hills and stunted trees, and water gardens. I remember one where there was water, steppingstones, trees leaning from the banks—and nothing else. These gardens are tranquil, and except for lotus in the water, most of them don't have flowers, just trees and bushes, moss and rocks and the natural or carefully altered contours of the earth. That is what most impressed my sister during her stay in Japan and her visits to the gardens—the quiet.

Until she came home and I spent an evening with her —first watching the boats sliding along the East River and the many lights, and then looking at the screen upon which she projected her memories—I'd never had anything but an idle wish to go to Japan. I'd like, as a matter of fact, to go everywhere, but this I'll never do. I have wished to go to China where my missionary grandparents labored and where my father was born. But looking at Esther's slides I began walking mentally in Japanese gardens through mist and rain, or pale sunlight, and marking the many shades of green, the velvet softness of moss, the hard, strengthening shapes of rocks, the flowing of water. I've been in orchid-hung Japanese gardens in Hawaii, but the ones on Esther's slides are different.

To be tranquil in a tranquil place, shut away from noise and clatter, to dream along a little bank and stoop to see the pattern of the living moss, must be a wonderful thing; the mind quieted and the need for hurry forgotten; serenity like a cool and gentle hand upon one's forehead.

Here on my imaginary terrace we can sit and look

across my imaginary fields, and later walk down to the brook which divides field from lawn, and cross the steppingstones to the other side.

Steppingstones are like experiences. Moving from one to another presents a certain amount of danger; you can slip if you don't watch where you are going.

On the steppingstones of experience we move from one phase of life to another. We can't remain indefinitely on any particular spot, however we may wish to; nor can we hurry across. It is no brook, which life long we cross, but a wide, mysterious stream. To keep one's balance is absolutely essential. And balance is almost the hardest thing in life to maintain.

Nature is all balance, however imbalanced she seems —too much rain here, too much snow there; floods or drought; she always seems to speak in extremes but actually, there's balance. When we interfere, sometimes the balance is lost; when we build great factories, for instance, the waste flows into rivers, rivers flow into oceans and many fish may die.

Preserving one's sense of balance on the steppingstones of experience is difficult. In any situation the balanced, objective view is the one which will bring us through eventually, but confronted with uncertainty and blinded by anxiety, it often seems impossible.

Some people liken living to a tightrope; most of us think of it as a path or road leading somewhere, but over what terrain we cannot judge; there are signposts but also long, unmarked, unlighted stretches. Stepping-stones constitute another kind of road; you pick your way from experience to experience, sometimes walking delicately like Agag, but sometimes forgetting that you mustn't hurry and often feeling that any moment dark waters will close over your head.

Now, because this is merely an imaginary excursion we can retrace our steps, as you can't in reality; you must go forward. But we can go back over our stones and reach the place from whence we started, cross the terrace, and enter the room called August.

August

August is a hold-your-breath month, usually with hot days and cooling-off nights. Here is where I mutter again about the louder mutter of thunder and the fork-tailed lightning. Forked lightning frightens me. When I summered on the St. Lawrence, it was astonishing to see a storm travel down the exact center of the river, rain on one side, no rain on the other; and terrifying to look across and see lightning strike a barn.

In this month it is as if the birds had already migrated. They haven't; they are just keeping cool and still where the leaves are thickest. Now and then the cardinal flashes past, red sealing wax on wings. Only at dawn and dusk do most birds sing, remembering their obligations in matins and vespers.

If we walk down to the trickle which, in spring, was white water flowing over rocks and spreading into meadows, we'll see how the grass has grown in it, and if you look at the pond, you'll find it full of algae. But almost always we can flush a pheasant and his wives from the thicket back of the stand of black alders.

At teatime, the birds revive and come to the mill-stone for a bath, and the fat doves are lazy in the burned-off grass. If there is any water in the pond, the mallards will fly in sometimes. And if a stranger bird intrudes, they'll waddle a considerable distance to the house and sit glumly in the bird bath; two fill it, one on either side. I've even met them rocking up the brick paths.

Sunburned youngsters and their parents are returning now from a holiday, or setting out on one. Commuters pant in the trains; cars whoosh past. And at night, when lights shine back of curtains, on city or village streets and on country roads and lanes there are lovers strolling, old and young, and children reluctantly heading for home. There's always someone walking a dog; an echo of laughter, a whistle, or a mother calling a child to supper or bed.

The stars are big in August and the moon is copper-gold. A while back a new small comet was sighted and named for its discoverer, Mrkos. If you can pronounce it, you are cleverer than I. There's an enchantment in thinking of a new light streaking across the sky. Or is it new? Do you suppose it was always there, waiting to be seen?

I marvel over stars. When I was nine, my grandfather gave me a book about them. My older granddaughter has it now. Perhaps she likes it. I didn't, although I loved Grandfather.

I wanted then, and I desire now, to think of the stars as pointed holes snipped in the distant canopy of the sky, polished by angels and affording us, when night falls and we look upward, a glimpse of celestial light.

The word *celestial* is one I've always loved. There are many others—*dusk* and *mist* and *twilight*—a long list, including the names of certain colors. But there is a special singing in the sound of celestial.

When, during the First World War, men flew, it was by celestial navigation. Ships, too, steered by stars. The instruments since invented and used make flying—and shipping—safer, but sometimes, when the instruments fail, pilot and navigator have to return to celestial navigation, which fortunately they've studied.

Often our personal instruments fail, those we have learned to use over the years: psychology, philosophy, a pattern of thinking; then, we have to steer by the stars.

This month we shall see the planets, and the moon waxing and waning; a silver splinter, a slice of lucent melon, a glowing round. Have you ever caught her in a mirror? I did once, as a girl standing in a little room which had one window. Dreaming abstractedly, I forgot to turn on the light, and picked up a mirror. And there she floated upon its surface, tiny and perfect, the full moon between my hands.

This month we will see the Perseids, the showers of meteors. That's what they're called. I call them shooting stars and, when I see them, I make a wish.

So many of my friends are chronically disturbed; they worry about wars, the stock market, the rising costs of everything and especially outer space. They talk incessantly of satellites, guided missiles, launching pads and missions to the moon. To my desk come innumerable letters concerned with the space age. But the writers forget the familiar spaces, the walls which hold in happy embrace the delight and responsibility of living upon our own relatively small planet.

When they worry, in conversation or with their pens, I wonder: Why are people so afraid? Oh, I know that time moves too quickly and we don't know what lies ahead. We never have, even in our personal lives. For us all, there are the hundred and one unexpected adjustments, the problems and pressures, and the persistent human fear of the unknown.

Yet, in a slower era when people were not as hasty either in hearts or minds, they looked up and out, in trust. When bad times came, they mended their fences, tightened their belts, said their prayers and moved forward.

I am unconcerned about the possibility that there may be people on other planets and I am not booking a trip to the moon. I haven't seen all of this small star yet, and I look upon the moon as an ardent magic in what I call the sky. I vaguely know of what materials the sky is composed but prefer to forget the information. This arching blue, this bend of brooding gray or black damask, this rose-gold glory at sunup or sundown, is for me sufficient. I am too interested in living right here—and simultaneously upon those spiritual planes which no scientist has yet explored or even named—to worry about outer space.

It lies all about us, above and around this house and the houses of friends and strangers. I do not feel uncomfortable knowing this.

The inner space, the home place of the spirit, the in-dwelling with God, profoundly concerns me. All I inwardly see and hear is as important to me as that which is outward: the tree stooped with wind, the descending rain, the bird flying upward, then dropping like a feathered stone to earth, and rising again.

Fear attracts fear; trust increases trust. My mother's mother used to say, "Prepare for the future, but never fear it." It's as good advice now as fifty years ago. Perhaps, better.

So let them go orbiting about the moon.

I've had a disappointment this month. I'd expected a visitor, a friend from Australia. I met her first on her sheep station in '39, and saw her again in Sydney in '54. I'd looked forward to Winnie's visit. It is always a joy to be with this woman, who has raised eleven children and become, in several fields, one of those quiet successes about which you aren't apt to read. She influences for good everyone who knows her.

She was a trained nurse and, I think, Irish born. Her Irish father was a bush doctor in Australia's back country, the never-never land. During the First World War she fell in love with and married a soldier patient. And after a while they had their first station and raised sheep —beautiful sheep—as well as wonderful children. When first I knew Winnie, she was, in a way, revolutionizing the wool industry.

She was also interested in the aborigines and in later years she's spent much time in the Northern Territory

—which is hotter than fire and a good deal wetter. My plane touched down at Darwin in '54. I had a couple of hours there in the rain and heat, and mentally took off the hat I wasn't wearing to Winnie.

Now that she can leave the running of stations to others—she's been a widow for some time—she visits the missions and has brought them many skills and much help. Usually she goes first to Darwin, where she just waits serenely until a plane comes in, bringing supplies for the missions. Then she gets aboard with the pilot and goes along.

I have thought about this a good deal. Most of us, being in such a swivet of hurry, want to get somewhere right away, tomorrow, today, even yesterday. I am not guiltless of this urge. And when we pray for something we say, in effect, *hurry*.

But you can't hurry God.

It's good to be like Winnie, waiting somewhere quietly and, while you are waiting, doing all you can to meet the day's needs and duties. After a while the plane will come along and the pilot, in His good time, will take you where He wishes you to go.

Winnie writes that she'll come next spring. She has a son in the States. So I can now look forward to April, but I can't hurry that either.

Artificial time is arbitrary, divided off on clock and calendar. . . . Here I go again, pondering on time. Can you tell me where yesterday went? Was there ever a yesterday, really? I don't think so because yesterday was once today and today is also tomorrow. I am writing this on Thursday and when Friday comes I'll ask: What shall I do *today?*

So it's always today. As I've said, I like to look back and also ahead—back to remember joy and also the lessons learned; ahead to whatever is there, wondering about it. But I am tired of people who live almost wholly in the future. Everything marvelous is going to happen then, they say, and meantime inch through today as best they can, without caring. They don't like the present. Those who live mainly in the past don't like it, either. Both are like children. One longs for the picnic ahead, around the unturned corner; and the other weeps for the picnic of long ago—forgetting no doubt, sunstroke, ants, rain.

Remember the television program, *See It Now?* There's never been better counsel. See it now: the world in which you live, the world around you. You don't have to travel to do it. Most of us are sensitive to beauty, and beauty is where you find it: in a city back yard, on a rooftop, in a park; in all the natural loveliness we see, whether from a train window, a car, or from the windows we call our own.

How many people do you know who are really mature? I don't know many and am not, myself, among them. It is almost impossible to believe that you are other than you were at eighteen, save physically. There, you have to admit the slowing down, the infirmities and the outgrown interest. But neither calendar nor mirror tell the whole story.

We learn as we grow older the language of the grownup, and accept responsibilities that, as children, we did not know existed. But all this seems almost imposed upon us, or perhaps overlays us like a patina. Often when I am talking to friends, or sitting here at the typewriter, and particularly when I am speaking from a platform—as I've been doing lately—I feel insecure; but also amused. Like the old lady in the nursery rhyme, I can't believe that this is I. I want to laugh at myself, for at such times I have the exact sensation I experienced when, as a child, I was permitted to dress up in my pretty mother's clothes and wear her high heels. The clothes didn't fit and I tottered shakily on the heels; but I was playing grownup.

Aren't most of us doing that, a great deal of the time?

This takes me right back to the steppingstones and the balance, for I believe that true maturity lies in balance; in acceptance and learning. Once we've learned a lesson we needn't go over it again, except to think of what it's taught us, in a refresher-course sort of way.

Maturity lies also in meeting each obligation as it

presents itself. In the informal speaking I do I come into contact with many church groups, large and small, of differing faiths and creeds, with a number of people interested in writing and with those in various clubs, both men and women. It has been my privilege to talk to people of other races. My over-all observation remains unchanged from year to year: there is a basic similarity in the everyday experiences of people, in their seeking, their terrors, their insecurities.

August, like July, is a month for holidays. Half my friends are somewhere else, most of them enjoying themselves to such an extent that, worn out with it, they'll come home and collapse gratefully in kitchen or office. In August, you can't put a needle between the sun bathers on a beach or the campers by the lakes and in the mountains. I think that August in Europe must be like a merry-go-round. I haven't been there during August since 1914 when I stood, silent on a hot night, above and beyond a roaring, hysterical mob milling about a railway station. I could hear them, but I was on a siding, watching quiet men as they lighted cigarettes, leaning from car windows to speak with someone on the platform. They were starting the journey to war from Saxony, which is in Germany.

Some of my friends take the upside down trips now,

and ski in, say, South America. I often wonder why people avoid the natural sequences of their local seasons? They flee to the South, to far-away islands in a New England winter, and during a New England summer they ski on the other side of the equator. Why can't they stay home, ski there in winter and toast themselves brown in summer? I don't know. There's a gay perversity about human nature especially if you have the wherewithal to indulge it; you want to be anywhere but where you are.

I am dreaming of England, of another trip there sometime. I don't know whether I'll make it or not, but half the pleasure lies in the dreams and the plans.

I have a friend who was eighty-four last winter. Her husband had died prior to her Leap Year birthday . . . and a little later she began to plan to go abroad with two loving members of her family. I don't know, as I write, whether she will or not, but, the plan's the thing.

You have to plan, I think: a trip, new decor, a dress for next Christmas (I haven't had a red dress in a long time), a fresh coat of paint on outside or inside walls. These things may never come to pass. Half a dozen things can knock a plan into a cocked hat—(a silly expression if ever I heard one), but to plan is to presume a future and to presume a future is to accept life, whether or not you ever put the plan into operation.

This I have learned the hard way. It took me almost

sixty years to do it: to plan, to presume—and then to adjust to alteration.

For instance, the picnic; so it rains when the baskets are all packed. The contents will taste just as good eaten at the kitchen table even if the view isn't as attractive.

Few things turn out quite as you plan them, and this can apply to anything—from your daughter's wedding to the roast in the oven.

When, a number of years ago, I woke one January morning and announced to myself and others, "I'm going around the world by plane next September fifteenth," no one could have been more surprised than I. This information must have been given to me in my sleep, for I had gone to bed with no more plans than to fly in the spring to Colorado to see my daughter Ann after brief visits in Chicago and Kansas City; and in the early summer to be with Gladys and Eleanor on the Cape for a while.

Yet I woke, and there the plan was—complete—even to what I'd do about the household I'd be leaving, the income tax and the clothes needed to meet rapid changes of climate.

So I went about getting a passport and being vaccinated and writing to people I wanted to see and booking flights and hotels, as if I were still in the dream.

This plan worked out to specification, but many do not, so we need to be flexible. We can always cancel tickets and reservations; the car can be put in shape later, and we can go wherever it is at another time, or even stay home.

I was born with an orderly mind and a sense of organization and it took me a while to learn to cancel, change, alter and rearrange. But it can be done.

My older daughter, Hervey, must have come in. I just heard someone wandering about the kitchen and the refrigerator door slam and ice tinkle in a glass. I wonder if she's gone out to pick some mint?

Yes.

A minute ago, she leaned over my shoulder and asked, "What are you writing about?" and I said, "August." She looked at the page, mistakes and all, and said, "So write about it," and went off with her iced-tea glass in her hand.

I correct my mistakes page by page and every time I do so I think, with pity and gratitude, of the patient typist who will retype it, and of my beloved friend and agent, Dorothy, who has to read my copy—several times. There are always mistakes. All mine.

Sometimes when readers write me, I answer and address the envelope incorrectly. I've never had a secretary and when it comes to handwriting, let alone typing, I'm about as efficient as a kitten with a pen or on the keys. So the letter comes back and then I worry.

I don't want anyone to think me unappreciative or rude. I answer those who write to me, even when they don't like what they've read. I'm sorry they don't, but they're entitled to their opinions.

So am I.

Now and then someone writes, "You don't make sense." There's one who says I don't make sense because I believe in God. She writes now and then to reproach me.

Well, I don't seek to convince or convert. I am just terribly sorry for anyone lacking faith in the divine plan and purpose, who has no belief in the universal power of prayer and none save herself in whom to trust.

There are others, men among them, who scold me for being an ancient Pollyanna, and implore me to become realistic.

These people miss so much. Maybe they're right, maybe I'm wrong. I don't think I am; but I'd rather be than lack the faith I now possess.

Hervey came in again to announce that the weatherman says it will rain tonight or tomorrow. Perhaps before supper. Clouds are piling up and a moment ago there was a roll on the thunder drums.

Yet in the night, the wind may change so that tomorrow we'll have another hot, flawless morning, with fat, white clouds too lazy to move far and dust rising from the road. The wind can change any time for us all, to bring storm after sun, or sun after storm. This storm may build up and break tonight, or decide to go out to sea, or it may arrive full-fledged before dawn as the noisy forerunner of hurricane weather.

We can't alter it; and if it rains, the earth will be grateful as will the listless leaves, the fainthearted brook. It won't rain forever, it never has; it didn't even for Noah.

"How's August going?" my daughter inquires.

"Almost gone," I reply.

She has tea for me, too, so I'll go and sit with her on the pink love seats and look at the painting of Diamond Head above the yellow flowers on the table. Lunar moths bumble against the screen door and window-panes, but I won't close the shutters yet. Before the storm, if we look out, we may see the shooting stars, and we can wish upon them.

Spring's sweet promise has been fulfilled, and summer's long days with their dramatics are flowing into early fall. Time is a circle; no end and no beginning.

Well, happy autumn at home or abroad and, wherever you are, the ability to say, "Thank you, Father, for this day and for whatever is to come in the days to follow."

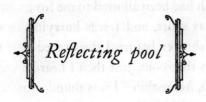

Reflecting pool

Somewhere on the terrace or patio let's have a reflecting pool and put pink lotus blossoms in it, for there is enduring magic about water. Did you know that in Eastern countries there are water diviners and ink diviners, too? The crystal ball is not the only method of foretelling the future. I once saw a sand diviner and have always regretted I didn't stop and ask what the sands held for me.

I think it was in Pakistan. That world flight, so long ago, has become a little dim. But there were two stops, during which we were taken off the plane, put in buses and taken to a hostelry for showers and refreshments. One was in Darwin, the other Pakistan.

Anyway, this sand diviner sat outside the door of the room which had been allotted to me for an hour.

Time was short, and I was hurrying so that I was under the shower before I discovered that the towels were across the room. Just then I heard a voice crying, "Memsahib, Memsahib." I was thunderstruck, for I had never in my wildest dreams thought anyone would address me as Memsahib—a word I've known since I started to read Kipling. Dripping my way to the door, I inquired who was there. It appeared that someone wanted to polish my shoes. They were not the polishable type and I returned to my shower.

When I came out, to walk down a long porch, I saw an old man squatting near the door. He had sand before him in some sort of receptacle, and was drawing lines in it. I've forgotten the words he spoke, but the meaning was: Would I like my future foretold?

I shook my head. I didn't know how long it would take or what currency he required in return, and so hurried away to join the other plane passengers for tea; then back to the bus and airport.

Although at that time I had presumed a future and was acting on the presumption, the thought of the future was, for me personally, an ache as the knowledge of the immediate past was a wound . . . . Now, however, I sometimes wonder what he would have told me?

Let us stand by the reflecting pool, clearer than any crystal and look into it. Water reflects everything about it—the sky, the stars, the moon, the nearby branches of trees, the faces of those who lean over to look into it.

Reflection is a lovely twofold word. A mirror reflects. So does calm water. When it is ruffled by the wind, the reflections are broken; they waver across the surface of pond or pool or river. And we reflect. In the dictionary sense this means a faculty of the human mind: ". . . a meditative thoughtfulness," says my bulky Oxford.

But the mind reflects more than the water does. The mind can reflect both the present and past. The water holds no shape of past reflections; it shows us only the now, the very moment.

Sometimes the mind, troubled by winds and sudden currents reflects past and present incompletely, brokenly, waveringly. At other times it is still, and sees the picture with clarity.

But like the pool, the mind cannot reflect the future. It can only reflect *upon* it.

Perhaps if we look into the reflecting pool on the terrace, the reflecting pools of our minds will encounter serendipity.

I have written elsewhere of serendipity, but it is too charming a conceit to be tarnished by repetition. This word, coined by Horace Walpole in 1754, is coming into use again. It derives from his allusion to a fantasy, "The Three Princes of Serendip" (which was the old name for Ceylon), in the course of which the princes were always making discoveries of things they weren't looking for—happy things, as well as unexpected.

Always in the reflections of our minds we are looking for reasons for what has happened or is happening; we are in search of answers. Perhaps we will chance on something lovely and unexpected, a thought leading us into paths we had forgotten or did not know were there.

What more can I wish you as we walk from August to September than serendipity in the next room?

September

Here in New England, September is spangled with surprise. I remember a Labor Day weekend years ago at the other house when the weather was hotter than any Fourth of July. We had house guests who sat around, panted, buried their noses in glasses of frosty drinks, and then went dutifully with us to an outdoor concert, where, under a clear, star-smitten sky, we listened to great music and slapped mosquitoes.

The next morning our friend, Marion, entered her husband's room and found him pitifully huddled beneath a chenille bath mat. The temperature had dropped umpteen degrees before dawn and I'd forgotten to put extra blankets at the foot of his bed. The mere thought of extra blankets would have sent me into a spin some hours earlier. All the other beds had them, though.

This episode I have never lived down and I'm certain such a sudden drop in temperature is the sort of surprise I could do without—even though the change was welcome—just as I can do without hurricanes, thank you. But no matter how many Septembers I witness, I am always amazed by their variety.

Memory is the strangest thing. Not long ago I tore a leaf from my calendar desk pad and I saw a notation for the next evening. Just a Christian name (a woman's) and an hour. As the hour was 7 P.M., I knew I had to go somewhere or that someone was coming here. Where? Who? I call few people by the name I had written on the pad. One lives near me. I telephoned her and asked, "Do we have a date?" The answer, gracefully expressed, was "No, but I'm awfully sorry." One lives in California. One is my agent and another, resident in Florida, a friend I haven't seen for nearly forty years.

"There must be a fifth," I said wildly.

I couldn't remember making any engagement, but

then the preceding weeks had been crowded, difficult and darkened by grief.

I went through my address book, which took me until the eleven-o'clock news. I couldn't face the telephone books. There are a lot of places around here, and I know people in most of them. On my way upstairs, I said aloud, "But the knowledge is somewhere in my consciousness. Please find it for me."

I had an appalling vision of sitting down to a solitary, early supper after the next day's work, and then suddenly remembering, leaping from the table and driving off in all directions, as Stephen Leacock said, for a second dinner. Or worse still, composing myself to read awhile before returning to work, after Gussie had gone home, and then hearing the door chimes and opening to one or more people all set for a happy evening.

Now, up the stairs I went and as I reached the door of my room, I remembered.

You may say it's absurd to believe that God is keeping your engagement book for you. Why? Nothing is impossible to Him; and perhaps He marks our going out and coming in more closely than we think.

But for several hours I'd worried.

I don't know how many of you who read this are worriers. Nowadays we don't talk much about worrying; we learnedly discourse on anxiety patterns and tensions. Everyone suffers from tensions; even our dogs take tranquilizers. But I'm just a plain old-fashioned worrier. I think of other peoples' worries as being dressed up. Mine wear calico and sunbonnets and side-laced boots.

I know worry is futile and destructive. In the last few years I've tried to do something about it. The only answer I can come up with, the sole method which has operated for me, is Trust. If there are other answers, I'll tell you when I find them; even the smallest solution helps.

I think I've always been somewhat proud of being well organized, but the other day, when I made a smug statement to that effect, a close friend said calmly, "Too well."

I am learning to employ less rigidity in organization. Time was when, if a little plan was altered—"Come Tuesday instead of Thursday," for instance—I was thrown out of gear like a small, determined machine that refuses to tolerate the speck of dust or whatever it is that throws things out of gear. And I realize now the tortures to which I subjected those close to me, insisting, as I did, that I had to get to a railroad station an hour before the train's scheduled departure. Now I allow myself reasonable time and no longer wait with my eyes pinned to the wall clock.

I fly a great deal these days, however, and airplane companies *like* organized people; they want you there ahead of time, so I don't feel guilty if I'm early. And if my seat isn't an assigned one, I march sedately to whatever gate will lead me to my wings, and hang over it. When it opens, I flee across the field as if pursued. Maybe I can conquer that, too; I'll have to, when I can no longer run.

I've rarely broken an engagement to speak locally or out of town; only when illness or disaster made it necessary. I haven't quite recovered from the embarrassment I felt when, some months ago, I had to break an appointment only a few hours before I was supposed to be in the city. But I couldn't call a television studio at one in the morning, which was exactly the time my virus had leaped at me, and took over, although I'd gone to bed feeling just fine.

Every season brings its gifts. The sumach reddens in September, and on Cape Cod the beach grasses dry to a rich, chocolate brown and the cranberry bogs flush into maroon.

It is the scallop season, too. As a child I went scalloping with my parents and someone told me that the little blue dots on the edge of muscle around the inside of the shells were the scallop's *eyes!* It's taken me the longest time not to believe it.

September gifts are special: the tawny apple, the purple grape, the leaves starting their succession of every shade of gold and wine. And particularly clouds.

Clouds are always wonderful, but something's added in autumn, whether or not there is reflecting water beneath them. During holidays at the Cape, I used to lie on a couch and watch for an hour or more the altering and drifting shapes. Sometimes they would darken, and hold a threat of wind or rain; sometimes they streamed away in mares' tails, and at dawn or before dusk they contained the essence of changing color.

Some time ago, a friend sitting next to me in a plane, looked down with me at the clouds massed beneath us, as the shadow of the wings moved over them. They were not static; they seemed as light as whipped cream, yet as firm as earth. They shifted in color, and I spoke to him of flying at night with a fog-bound earth under me and heavy clouds, but, where I was, brilliance, for a dark sky can be brilliant and this one had a shining moon and a million stars.

My friend asked idly, "Have you ever really thought about the top side of a cloud? It's always bright."

It's all in the viewpoint. Walking our separate, often difficult paths, our vision is often restricted. If the cloud above us is dark, it obscures the sun and we cannot see over and above it. I still, I'm afraid, drudge and fuss along, shrinking from a falling barometer and the menace of a storm which hasn't broken—and possibly never will.

The top side of the cloud isn't the proverbial silver lining. It's much more. The silver lining has always meant to me a compensation for something which has happened; such as, the barn burned down but no one was injured. Figuratively, the top side of the cloud symbolizes the attitude by which you can see through a dark situation to the other side and the sunlight.

No person with the usual human problems, none who loves, none who lives can emerge one hundred per cent topside. But we can try.

Some years ago I was on a television program which originated from this house. I'm not nervous on radio, TV or lecture platforms any more, but this type of program was new to me, and I was alone during my part in it. I had to go from room to room, downstairs. For two weeks the house and grounds were overrun by technicians, and on the night of the telecast there were dozens of men swarming about, batteries of lights, cameras, switchboards and such. I know a little about television; it's a tense business and anything can go wrong. Tension is contagious, so I told myself I wouldn't feel it, for if I did, the people who did the real work would be doubly on edge.

Two days before the show, my older daughter was in an automobile accident. She wasn't hurt; no one was, but the car was hopelessly damaged. After she telephoned me about it, I didn't hear from her for twenty-four hours. When the day of the program arrived, I was almost mindless from worry. And then I thought suddenly: *Let go*.

She was all right; that was the important factor.

By letting go, I don't mean relaxing. It's different. When you let go, you not only loosen the tautness and the tension, you are also grateful for the silver lining, for the top side of the cloud where it is serene and you can assure yourself: It's happened, it's over, no one is the worse for it. Let go.

As for relaxing, I suppose it's heresy, but I am tired of friends, strangers and the writers of books who harp on relaxing. We can't become a nation of rag dolls. It is necessary for character growth to have, and meet, problems; even to worry; even, sometimes, to fear, as there are fears which are salutary—but never to worry or fear in excess. If, by working at it constantly, we can attain an inner source of refreshment and trust, putting our difficulties in God's hand, but at the same time recognizing that He requires us to do something about them also, we have taken a long step ahead. It sounds inconsistent and perhaps impossible, but you can almost fly to pieces on the surface and still maintain your citadel of durable inner calm.

It has been said for hundreds of years that most of us

squander Time's good coin worrying about what might happen—and doesn't—as well as about what has happened, which can't be remedied. Look, for instance, at the speaking engagement I had to break. I'm sure the powers in charge scurried around to find someone to take my place and that there were fifty, ready, able and willing. The important thing to me was the keeping of my promise; I have in my lifetime broken at least two grave promises—perhaps that's why I now try harder not to. But aside from the fact that I couldn't be where I'd said I'd be, due to twenty-four-hour collywobbles, it wasn't really vital.

If you made a list of the things you believe are vital to you, and then sat and looked at it, I'm sure you'd cross off a number of items, leaving only a few necessities. I've listed these elsewhere as common to us all. I'll do it again.

Love, worship, work; a roof over your head, food on your table.

Under love, come all the human relationships and your essential relationship with God; under worship, the need for prayer, which is a tuning in to strength and the security of the spirit; under work, I suppose the need is for tasks which give you joy. The necessities of life are a sort of subheading; for these you usually have to work.

I haven't listed happiness as a need by itself. If you

have the rest, you have that, too. I haven't listed play because anyone who works knows the twin need is recreation.

When my youngest granddaughter was two, she celebrated her birthday, and her father's fell on the following day. Her mother later reported to me that the baby went about on both days, observing the gifts, hers and her father's, and remarking, "Happy, happy, happy, *too*."

This may not denote much of a vocabulary, but it came from the heart.

Not long ago I learned that she, her small brother and parents went to visit near where they live in Florida. There was a beach, but it was too cold to swim. (I hope the C. of C. won't mind a ᶠactual statement.) However on their way home, the girl child remarked, "Everybody had fun."

This is a good way to grow up, being happy "too," wanting "everybody" to have fun.

One of the things which tires me is the earnest way people tell you not only to relax, but that money can't buy happiness. Not long ago I was concerned with a material problem, and a friend of mine said carelessly over the phone, "So what? It's only money!"

Well, I know money can't buy a great many things, but it does have purchasing powers. It can buy happiness for other people and that reflects like the sun on the giver. The little or much we give to alleviate human suffering, when thought of in less impersonal terms, can buy rejoicing; it can save minds and bodies, clothe and feed, shelter and warm.

We know it is more blessed to give than to receive, and it can often be more pleasurable. Yet when you hear people say—I've heard it—"Of course, I'm naturally a giver, I love to give," take it with a large grain of salt. For there is in such a statement the little Jack Horner attitude— What a good boy am I! The truly selfless person does not stop to think about his giving; he does it as naturally as he breathes. Nor does he consider anything a sacrifice, for he operates in love and nothing is a sacrifice when love is the motivation. But those who harp continually upon their sacrifices forget that every sacrifice demands an altar and do not know that theirs are offered upon the altar of the ego. And I don't mean alter-ego!

I have known many selfish people; many who believed themselves to be unselfish, and many who were, by my standards really so. But few who were selfless.

I can count *them* on the fingers of my hands. One of them was a friend born on St. Patrick's day; another was Eleanor.

How I wish I could go through an ordinary working, playing, resting day without committing thoughtlessness, without having done a selfish thing, spoken or thought an unkindness, an untruth, a criticism. So far, I haven't ever succeeded. You'd think that in the handful of hours which make up a waking day one could accomplish that much if only just once. But I haven't.

It is not that I aspire to sainthood—only that I'd like to be better than I am. Maybe the trying counts.

In the almost forty years I've been a professional writer, many people have written me, of all ages, and from many places—some have written for twenty-five years or more, though we have never met—and I am continually astonished by the sheer goodness of what we call an average person. Oh, among the letter writers there are those who take pen in hand to beg; they want the mortgage paid off, a college education, or advice on everything from how to hold a husband to how to write a novel. There are multitudes who "just know" that they are a shade different from brother and neighbor. Believe in your own uniqueness and in your ability to give, to accomplish, to leave something, for it is only by the small steps of the individual that the world moves forward.

There have always been, there are now, many human minds accounted brilliant, and even great, which have expressed themselves in terms of disillusionment and cynicism, in terms of denial and doubt. These minds believe in nothing, not even in themselves. These are the minds which, however great, somehow reach out to strangle.

I often think of things that strangle, and some are beautiful—as are the words of some of the cynical writers. For instance, the great wisteria outside the study windows, under an immense maple. This bush is too big to move, its roots are as those of a tree. I love it, but we watch it carefully in the spring before and after the great mauve flowers droop downward, spilling their fragrance. For the little tendrils have a way of creeping up, and out, and binding around the maple branches. There are many vines which, stealthily and mutely choke the life from trees, as surely as the weeds rise silently to cut off air and nourishment from flowers. Some of the vines and weeds are inconspicuous; others, lovely to see.

Cynicism and distrust of man's innate goodness and of his Creator, no matter how superbly written or spoken, are stranglers.

The common terms we often use—"clinging vine" and "stranglehold"—have much meaning.

Look with me at the clouds. With our vision we can't see the top side from here. But whatever shapes the clouds assume in our limited sight, let them not, for us, portend anxiety or storm, knowing as we do that top-side there is beauty, order and peace.

{ Moon gate }

It is my fancy to write of thirteen months. In a book, a year can have thirteen months, can it not? During one's lifetime a single year sometimes seems to stretch to ten, and at another time to be only a few short weeks, depending on events, outward and inward.

So, in this year, we have two Octobers. . . .

We have been walking across patio and terrace; this time, I propose a courtyard. They have similarities, but a patio is not always *enclosed;* I've seen, I think, only one with four walls; and a terrace is usually open on at least one side. But our courtyard is of Chinese design. It can even be many courtyards, such as the large families of means in Old China built to shelter innumerable sons, wives, children, serving people.

These great houses were walled, foursquare. To enter the first courtyard there was usually a door with a peephole in it; to enter other courtyards you went through gates. Most of them were named, as my grandmother often told me, and as the Quaker writer, Nora Waln, tells us in her lovely book *The House of Exile*. I have not reread it for some years, but at the time I was writing *American Family*, I collected many books relative to China—history, factual, fiction and memoirs. I vividly recall one gate of which Nora Waln spoke, The Gate of Compassion; if I remember correctly, this was the gate to which beggars came for food and help.

Moon gates I have seen. In Chinese gardens, fashioned by Chinese gardeners in Hawaii, for instance, there are little moon gates, so-called because of the carving on their panels.

I think we will go into our second October—as it is fanciful—through the Moon Gate. Or do you prefer the Gate of Compassion or that of Meditation? There must be small niches in these for Kwan Yin, Goddess of Mercy, bringer of quietude.

There should be a Gate of Understanding, also.

To be merciful, to ponder on the known world and

the implications of the unknown, these are essential in any month.

More and more as we move from one decade to another—and, in a sense, these are also gateways—we "understand" people. Almost anyone who reads is exposed to lay psychology—sometimes with rather unfortunate results. But there are also books written for those who would be more than laymen, public lectures to mixed audiences, and a spreading knowledge of philosophies, old and new—if anything is ever really new —and, of course, advancement in psychiatry. Practically everyone has a grasp of some of the terms and phrases, for they have passed into the language.

A couple of generations ago no one talked about complexes—an almost outworn term now—nor did we speak of frustrations, transference or ambivalence, to say nothing of other learned labels.

The understanding accorded a patient by his psychiatrist is arrived at through long, arduous and specialized training. The method—with or without a surface knowledge acquired from books—through which one person understands another is something else again; many factors enter into this: experience, relationship, and the mind and heart of him who understands. I have often heard people say, "I understand him perfectly."

No one understands another "perfectly," not even, I venture to say, the psychiatrist. Perhaps we would not appreciate perfect understanding; it would be at such variance with the understanding we accord ourselves.

No. Perfect understanding is an attribute of God.

But some people possess, inborn, what, for want of a better term, I call "spiritual understanding." It's not based on anything you can name; not psychology or common sense; not intelligence, or the search for motivations; not even love. For although the instinct and desire of love is to understand the beloved, there are veils we cannot remove from the image, and perhaps, do not wish to remove.

Spiritual understanding operates in quiet, and only occasionally manifests. It must cross many courtyards in order to reach the dwelling place of the mind. It comes in glimpses, it penetrates in momentary light. How often have you looked at someone you know, someone you think you understand as no one else ever could, and been aware of something you haven't known, something perhaps contrary to all you thought you understood?

Spiritual understanding, however barricaded against the reasoning mind by external factors is not confined to illuminating the people we love. It is a universal reaching out and encompassing. It is, in the moments we experience it, as if an infinitesimal spark from the light of God's All-Knowing had touched us.

When we try—and most of us do—to understand another—his needs, his difficulties, his character, why he does this or that, and what inspires or manacles him—we make the effort with our limited minds, and often with the loving, unlimited heart. I think we ought also to pray that we may, however briefly, understand him spiritually, which will open another gate, leading to a further dimension.

I have been meaning all along to put a bird feeder somewhere. I forgot it on patio and terrace, but I don't see why it can't be in a courtyard. We can call the gate nearest it the Gate of the Pausing Bird.

And even as the birds come, pause and are fed; so we also come, briefly, to the houses of our individual lives, there pause, and are fed.

There are more insignificant-looking birds than brilliant; there are more whose song is not unusual and these are hardly noticed. They come to our feeders here and with them often the quarreling and strident.

Not all of us can wear a red coat or yellow cap; not all can sing until the listening heart must break; not all are strong enough to fight for their share of grain.

Yet, each has wings, and he who marks the sparrow's fall marks also ours and our rising again, whether or not the flight is steady.

So fly with me now through the Moon Gate into an October not yet here.

October

This is a room I have not as yet entered. I do not know what it looks like, but I think that, outwardly, it will be beautifully furnished with living flame and ceilinged, mostly, with blue. I believe there will be fall-blooming roses. Last October, Gussie brought me bouquets of late blooms from a friend's garden. These roses do not last as long as summer's, in the house—at least they didn't for me—but they are sweeter than the spring and summer flowers; they have a special glory of color and scent.

There will be the little mums and the big, exhibiting courage before frost; and there will be birds, wondering if they'd like to stay all year or follow their relatives south.

Of course, we sometimes have disturbing visitations in October: floods, for instance, and sometimes early snow. But, taking an average, I would say that this October will be much as usual outdoors.

I know that the anniversary of my birth will fall upon the first day.

Where I shall be, what I shall be doing, what will disturb or make me happy, whether my work will progress, what will be my childrens' problems, I haven't the slightest idea. I have no sand diviner sitting outside the farmhouse door. I do not possess a crystal ball. The only time I've looked into one, which belonged to a friend, I didn't see anything. I cannot lay out cards, or read my own small square palm; nor have the stars in their courses, read by my astrologist friend, always foretold accurately. No gypsy crosses my path.

Nevertheless there are those—some I know well—who have what we call extrasensory perception. In a slight degree I have it myself, very slight. I do not believe, however, that we are intended to know, mile for mile, what lies ahead on the road. But occasionally, only a little way ahead. Whatever the ESP gift, it is usually given to illuminate a step just taken or the one we're about to take.

I do not think I'd want to know, entirely; I'm sure we were not meant to, wholly.

Few people could face with equanimity the certain knowledge of their own grave illnesses or deaths, or those of people they love, who are at the moment in excellent health. But when the unexpected lightning rips the roof from the secure dwelling we are given, I believe, another kind of ESP—the essential extra strength and power.

It is human nature to hope against hope; but when the dark, lonely moments come we are somehow armored to meet them.

Where shall I be in this thirteenth month through which I haven't yet lived? With whom?

I do not know. I know nothing beyond the fact that I'll be somewhere, on this earth; or, beyond it.

There has long been a movement to divide the year evenly into thirteen months; which would we're told, simplify everything—holidays, salaries and planning. So far it's come to nothing.

What is certain is that there *will* be a thirteenth month. As I began this book with the month of October, my second October should start another new year. Let it stand—a new year or an augmented old one.

Thank you for coming with me through the house of a year, with its extra room, and many happy returns of my unreached birthday.

One thing I know as surely as I know that the sun always rises and sets; I shall walk through the thirteenth month with trust. This has been, as I have called it, a Testament of Trust; for trust will take us through any month and any year.

I can't write about what will be happening around me in the thirteenth month. I know the pheasant will be in his fall plumage and when the time for hunting season closes in, I pray that he will find cover. I'm sure I'll buy new gourds and pumpkins and that at October's end the small imps and ghosts will come trick-or-treating to my door.

I'm convinced that Columbus Day will come. Very dear friends of mine, who were married on that date, used to say, "Wasn't it kind of the powers that be to set aside our wedding anniversary as a holiday?" And a little later there will be attacks upon the eardrums from the streets as we near the elections and trucks bearing loud speakers go by.

These things come with every October. But in each there will be events which haven't occurred before: new sharings and interests, new problems and, for ourselves and our friends, new happiness.

We can, during that part which repeats itself, walk

out in brilliant, mellow sunshine and observe the stubborn leaves. The pheasant, I am certain, will skid across the lawn into the tawny stubble of the meadow and the birds will tune up. There should be water in the pond and we can walk softly in order not to frighten the ducks who won't leave us until it ices over. And we can look up through the twisted branches of the ancient apple trees, bare by October, and see the sky.

What shall we look for in it—the moon, the star, the promise? Whatever it is, let's not look for fear.

A natural pearl is formed when the oyster is irritated by a grain of sand. Some pearls are small, some large; they vary in color and many are oddly misshapen. In such a way is character formed by irritation and disappointment, frustration and the large grains of sand which spell grief and tragedy. As in the natural pearl the layers of nacre are uneven. But I wonder if, when we reach our ultimate destination, the human spirit does not wear a necklace of pearls, which is judged for weight and beauty by our Creator?

As you know, I like shells. Here I can show you not only the oyster shells in the dining room but in the lacquer cup and on lacquer trays, on the Pembroke table under the painting of a Cape Cod scene; many others. Here's one from the coast of Scotland. There are several from Hawaii (which doesn't abound in them), and from Cape Cod and St. Thomas, Nassau and Jamaica. From the Captiva and Sanibel, and many which were sent to me from the Philippines.

There are also small branches of coral. I found one piece myself wading out from St. Thomas Beach, the antler coral; under water it was the most lovely mauve; now it is soft brown having perished out of its element.

Here's a big one. Put it to your ear and hear the spirit of the sea.

Wherever this October finds or takes us, God bless us there, you and me.

Vow

(For G.T.)

I will trust, through darkness, light
In risen suns, beyond the night;

I will trust, in claws of pain,
The Word which makes me whole again;

I will trust, in bitter grief,
Acceptance of the fallen leaf;

And though I find my heart in tears
I'll trust the months, I'll trust the years;

The Bread, the Staff, the Oil, the Rod,
The quiet Love and Will of God.